PENGUIN BOOKS

THE PENGUIN METAPHYSICAL LIBRARY
General Editor: Jacob Needleman

MY LIFE WITH A BRAHMIN FAMILY

Lizelle Reymond was born in the early part of this century in Neuchâtel, Switzerland. As a child, she traveled widely with her parents and enjoyed an extensive private education in art, music, and literature. When she was twenty, she became a librarian at the League of Nations, a post she held until World War II. After the war, she left Europe for Calcutta to begin the long series of Indian experiences that have inspired so much of her writing. Upon her return to the West in 1954, Madame Reymond joined groups studying the philosophy of G. I. Gurdjieff, chiefly in Paris and later in New York. Today she leads similar study groups in Geneva, her present home.

D0807150

LIZELLE REYMOND

My Life With a Brahmin Family

TRANSLATED FROM THE FRENCH BY LUCY NORTON

PENGUIN BOOKS INC

Baltimore · Maryland

Penguin Books Inc
7110 Ambassador Road
Baltimore, Maryland 21207, U.S.A.

Ma Vie Chez Les Brahmanes first published by Flammarion 1957
This translation first published by Rider and Company 1958
Published in Penguin Books 1972

Printed in the United States of America
by Kingsport Press, Inc.

THE PENGUIN METAPHYSICAL LIBRARY

The PENGUIN METAPHYSICAL LIBRARY offers books that can recall in modern man the forgotten knowledge of how to search for himself, knowledge he has lost in his haste to make himself comfortable in the world. From the most diverse geographical origins and historical periods, and from a wide variety of traditions and literary forms, the editor has selected for this series books that have the common goal of orienting man in the search for consciousness.

Throughout the Western world, the realization is dawning that contemporary science, including psychology, provides nothing for man that can take the place of the struggle for self-knowledge, and that most of our present religions have cut themselves off from the energy in their original teachings. Thus a great many Westerners are now seeking out ancient and modern texts that consider human life within cosmic schemes more purposeful than the universe of modern science.

But the understanding of how to relate these writings to our own lives remains elusive. Even the most serious and best informed among us are not sure which ideas are important and which are unnecessary for a real inner search to begin. Therefore, out of this flood of esoteric, traditional, and mystical writings, the editor has chosen only material that bears on the aim of looking impartially and with fresh hope at the chaos we see within ourselves and in the world around us.

JACOB NEEDLEMAN

Contents

Introduction

$\mathcal{M}$ ANY WESTERNERS HAVE TRAVELED TO INDIA, BUT FEW have returned with anything of concrete value for the West. The mere presence in our culture of sacred ideas from the Hindu religions does not seem enough to help us experience the simple truth about ourselves. As the younger generation now turns to the religions of Asia, and as spiritual teachers coming here from the East bring us practical techniques as well, the question arises whether these techniques may further distract us and make our lives even more opaque.

While writing and studying in India, Lizelle Reymond found her way into a world that few Westerners have ever seen. So rare is it for a European to live with a Brahmin family that her Indian friends advised her against it. Yet only by accepting this challenge was she able to discover something crucial about the preparation that is necessary, if sacred ideas and methods are to be instruments of real inner growth.

A Brahmin family is both a spiritual and a social unit. In this book, Lizelle Reymond reveals the events that led her to discover what this blending of the spiritual and the social means. More, rather than less, of herself had to be engaged and exposed in the day–to–day tasks of living. Every aspect of life, no matter how mundane or light–hearted, became a crucible wherein her wish for truth might suddenly be tested to the limit.

Surrounded by the rigorous outer forms of orthodox Hindu life—a life in which every gesture has meaning—she suffered all that it entails not to be able to "belong" to the community in which one lives. She constantly had to feel her own way to a more subtle and concrete understanding of her place, both as a member of the family and as a companion in search of inner reality. Whether teaching the children music or sorting rice, or trying to deal with servants who misunderstand her, she finds that the forms and rituals liberate her search even as they constrain her actions. They constantly remind her that she has failed to respond from the whole of herself.

"The family presents the environment through which Divine Power best finds its way," she is told. "There it can work, penetrating gradually into our minds, hearts, bodies and blood . . ." Measured against this approach to the whole of life, the current interest in esoteric ideas and practices is brought down to earth in a healthy fashion. Only after an extended period of living with her family was Madame Reymond prepared to study under a master who imposed upon her an even more subtle austerity in a remote Himalayan hermitage.*

My Life with a Brahmin Family thus gently and indirectly brings us to question our reasons for turning to esoteric ideas and methods. Could it be in order to avoid seeing the truth about our inner lives? We, too, live in a "family" and are constrained at every step by forces and conditions that seem to obstruct our freedom. What would be necessary for these very conditions to become the material by which we might come to know ourselves? Is it only powerful ideas and practical methods that we need? Surely, our first step, without which such help from outside may be wasted on us, is to risk being still, psychologically, in the place we find ourselves, so that the sensation of our own existence may appear, and with it the knowledge that we do not really know with whom we "belong" or why we are here.

* Her experience with this master and a presentation of his teachings have been published under the title *To Live Within* (Doubleday and Co., Garden City, 1971).

Foreword

For several months of the six years, from 1947 to 1953, which I spent in India, I lived in a Brahmin home as a member of the family, after which experience I went on to share the life, in the Himalayas, of one of those hermit-teachers, who are the guardians of wisdom. Alas! It is not possible to dwell upon the mountain-tops for ever. Sooner or later one must return to earth.

The Brahmins with whom I lived were strictly bound by the orthodox tradition, but at the same time, were well aware of the problems of living in a modern world. The older members of the family, it is true, held somewhat aloof, observing the development of our materialistic Western civilization from afar, but their sons, all university undergraduates or students at technical colleges, came daily into contact with Europe and the United States and were eager to learn to supply their country's needs. Republican India must find some way of reconciling these diametrically opposite and divergent trends, if the ancient traditions are to accept the laws laid down by the new constitution. A split between the two trends could mean the disintegration of India, as each side fully recognizes.

The family life of my Brahmin friends has not changed for thousands of years. It is still subject to a rigid discipline that has allowed India's religious heritage to be preserved intact. War, invasion, foreign occupation, partition, and modern progress have never disturbed it. It will remain unshaken through all the changing forms that the future may bring. Among the élite of India, some will always be found ready to make great personal sacrifices in order to keep the Tradition alive. The Rule which they follow in private, even when they seem to live like Europeans or Americans, is recognizable by a quality that is hard to define because at first its standards are unfamiliar. None the less, in their home lives, Yoga, that firm support in the quiet, methodical pursuit of true knowledge, plays the same vital and traditional part in ordinary everyday actions as in the austerities practised at great Yogic centres.

The home-life of my Brahmin family formed a unity from which no part could be subtracted. For a time, I had my own place in that life. Only one thing could have driven me from the family circle, disobedience to my own personal rule; in other words, had I been dishonest with myself for good or ill.

This story begins when I had been living for seven months in the little Himalayan town of Kurmachala, where I had gone to write and study, after spending more than two busy years at Calcutta, my first home-town amid the splendour and equalor of Bengal.

1

Panditji's First Visit

THE COLD WEATHER HAD COME AND THE TIBETANS were beginning to bring their flocks down from the hills, the goats heavily laden with borax. I could hear the strange sound of the bells with wooden clappers when they were still a long way off. When they passed my house, they were herded together by big Bhotian sheepdogs, looking half-crazed with exhaustion. At the head of the flocks walked highland shepherds, with the quiet dignity of mountain peoples, everywhere.

One evening, when my servant, Singh, brought me my lighted oil-lamp, he said that I had Hindu visitors, my first since the day seven months earlier when I had rented the Gauri villa, a little way from the town. Singh had shown my guests into the living-room, making it very plain that he knew them by his immensely formal manner of announcing their arrival. I went in and found two gentlemen waiting to see me. The younger, a man of about forty-five, introduced himself. He was Panda Vidyasagar, of Shanti Bhavan, and his companion was the family acharya, his private chaplin, responsible for the right conduct of his entire family.

Pandit Pandya lost no time in explaining their visit. 'We hear,' he said, 'that you are shortly going to leave us. Before you go, I should like you to meet my mother and take a meal

9

with me. Will tomorrow morning at half-past ten be con-
venient?' Then, giving me no time to answer, he immediately
began to explain at great length how to find his house, although, as he well knew, I passed it every time I went to the
town. Indeed, he must often have seen me, just as I had seen
him walking in his garden, which was famous for its roses
throughout the entire district. Finally, he said that he would
send an escort for me and make arrangements for my own man
to eat with his servants. In the face of such ultra-careful preparation, I could think of no suitable reply and simply smiled
in order to gain time, for I did not know his code of good manners. What I did know, however, was that it was a privilege
to be invited to pay my respects to the Mother of Shanti
Bhavan, the House of Peace.

There followed a long silence, during which I managed to
steal a sly glance at the chaplain—inscrutable expression, very
large nose, at least eighty years old, long slender hands like
carved ivory. He seemed to be standing on a solid base of two
enormous black buckled shoes, and I thereupon privately nick-
named him "Cyrano in Galoshes". The silence grew more and
more oppressive, but I had learned enough to know that it
must on no account be broken by a woman. Then something
strange happened, for those two men received me into the very
heart of their stillness, as though we had met in a relationship
predetermined by most explicit traditional laws.

When at last Pandit Vidyasagar spoke again, his voice was
friendly and informal as if we had known one another for a
long time. His whole tone had changed as well as his manner.
Then it was that I realized that he was fully informed of all
my actions and movements throughout the summer, and had
taken careful note of them. Everything that I had done had
been faithfully reported to him, down to the smallest detail.
But by whom? And why? He knew, for instance, where I had
come from, and who had been to see me, what I had bought
in the bazaar, and what temples I had visited. Someone had

told him the kind of food I ate at my main meal, so that he knew that all through the summer no one in my house had tasted meat or eggs. This final touch rather amused me because, although I had given Singh the freedom of the kitchen, he had turned out to be a past-master in the art of cooking and I had had nothing to complain of. Neverthless, I was careful not to seem surprised, although I must admit to feeling somewhat annoyed at this very frank way of announcing that he had been spying on me. After all, I reflected, the result was a great saving of time, since my guest evidently did not regard me as a stranger.

Later, speaking of himself, Pandit Vidyasagar said, 'I have four sons, a great blessing that has been vouchsafed to me in return, perhaps, for my self-sacrifice. That may well be, indeed, since it was never my wish to found a family. I happened, however, to be the only son of the elder branch, and my uncles ordered me to marry when I was only nineteen. One day I will show you the table of our *gotra*, which roughly corresponds to your family tree, and you will see that my sons are the twenty-ninth generation in the direct line.'

I did not know what to answer, but after a short pause, Pandit Vidyasagar burst out laughing, saying, 'Very soon, *Bahin* (sister), I shall have earned my retirement, for I have been head of the family almost from my birth. My father died when I was only a few months old.'

Thus, I learned that the Mother of Shanti Bhavan, whom I was to meet on the following day, had lived a widow's life of self-sacrifice and mortification for more than forty years and that Pandit Vidyasagar, her son, had been brought up like a prince, subject to no law, except that which the family-priest enforced to maintain the dignity of his position and ensure that the inner life of the whole family should revolve around him as its head.

Before they left, Pandit Vidyasagar asked me to show him the little room in which I worked, my typewriter and books, my notes and dictionaries. Was it really true, he said, that I had sent a parcel of manuscript to New York costing forty-eight rupees in stamps? The postman had gossiped about it in the bazaar. During all this time the priest had said nothing. He now walked silently away, leaning heavily on a walking-stick with a gold knob.

2

My First Visit to Shanti Bhavan

On the following day, punctual to the minute, I appeared at Shanti Bhavan with my two escorts, Naraïn, Pandit Vidyasagar's Brahmin servant, and Singh, my own retainer. He was of lower caste and therefore had to walk slightly behind Naraïn, which, however, did not prevent them from arguing the whole of the way in loud shrill voices, thus completely spoiling the walk for me.

Shanti Bhavan is one of a number of manor-houses built in the Nepalese style for Brahmins who came to settle in the highlands at the time of the Mongol invasions. According to local tradition, such houses have "souls" of their own. This one was sited with great care to face due north, and was planned in exact conformity with the rules laid down in the *Shastras*,[1] prescribing the relationship of angles, the thickness of walls, the height of doorways and the number of windows. At all times of day, the sunlight falls on one or other of the cornerstones, and within the house itself, the Holy Place, where the *pujâ* or service of adoration is held each morning, occupies the same place as the heart within the human body.

As time went on, a veranda, a room, and a gallery had been added whenever one of the sons had married and started a

---

[1] The *Shastras:* The Holy Writings of the Hindus, very ancient texts, regulating every aspect of human life.

family, and all of them had been planned according to the prescribed rules. Nothing was built haphazard, with the result there was an appearance of unity, despite the irregularities. Even details such as the small carved columns of the window-frames and the high treads of the stairs were in the same symbolical tradition.

The tall stone entrance and the great white surrounding wall had a forbidding look, like the keep of a mediaeval castle. All the charm of the house lay in the fact that some of the paving-stones in the courtyard had been replaced by rose-bushes, an unheard of luxury in that region, where every can of water had to be fetched from the communal well. Pandit Vidyasagar, however, loved roses, and liked to grow them. The entire house shone with a fresh coat of lime-wash, for the walls had been repainted only six months earlier, in honour of the Festival of the Lights. The dead whiteness served to bring out the colour of the wooden shutters with their tiny open-work grilles over narrow double windows.

All my nervousness vanished when I saw two young men, obviously strangers to the valley, who were playing with a tiger-cub on a lead. Pandit Vidyasagar stepped quickly forward and performed the introductions. The young men, it seemed, were devotees of Swâmi Narayâna, and lived with him in his *ashram*,[1] on the borders of Tibet. They were taking the tiger as a present from the Swâmi to the zoological gardens of Bombay. It was a magnificent creature and came purring up to me to rub its back against my sarî. Indeed, I learned to know it best of the three, for it was like a huge tame cat with vast claws that closed gently over my whole hand, and it soon fell asleep on my lap, making little mewing noises of utter contentment.

Panditji watched me for some time, and finally said,

---

[1] *Ashram:* A band of disciples who live with their spiritual director. A *swâmi* is a monk.

'Bahin, that animal is about to lose its freedom. If it had the least flicker of imagination and could realize what was happening, it might willingly exchange freedom for awareness. Then its cage could become a perfect ashram, where it would have everything it needed to achieve its aim. But since it is totally unaware, it will die of boredom. Do not let yourself be sentimental, Bahin, that would be quite wrong, for you would lose vital energy. You have chanced to meet at one of life's cross-roads, that is all. Come, let us go in and have something to eat.'

We entered a pleasant room that might have been designed for a number of purposes, office, store-room, library, or bed-room. It contained a plank-bed, books piled up on the floor, sacks of rice, a writing-desk covered with account books, and, on the walls, valuable Tibetan scrolls hanging side by side with chromolithographs of the household gods, scch as one sees in all Hindu houses.

Two brass trays had been placed on a low table, at which Panditji and I proceeded to sit down. Naraïn appeared at once, looking quite different, for he was wearing nothing but an immaculate, white silk skirt draped around his loins, and his Brahmin cord cross-wise over his chest. He also wore a neck-lace of amulets, and a bracelet on the upper part of his left arm. He waited on us with quiet, unhurried movements, keep-ing one eye on me all the time, in case I should make any so-cial blunders. If ever I seemed to hesitate over a dish, he at once placed in front of me the fruit or vegetable which I ought to take next. It was a strictly vegetarian meal, consist-ing largely of lentils, either fried or in a purée, dressed with various sauces.

Panditji was not paying any attention to me. At last he said abruptly, 'You are the first foreigner ever to enter this room. I shall now take you into the drawing-room, where my mother will receive you, but I think I should warn you that like all the other women in this family she observes a very strict discipline, whereas I, although I follow it in a very real sense, am also much interested in the different conceptions of the Divine Essence. These ideas are sometimes extremely muddled, but the most primitive and savage religious practices are often an expression of purely abstract ideas. With your Christian upbringing you may not be capable of grasping this truth, but whereas the masses may need things which they can touch and see and that their other senses can appreciate, the men of my caste are all students of the *Veda*.'[1]

When we had finished eating, Naraïn poured water over our hands, and Panditji led me out on to the terrace. He swept his hand along the line of the horizon, saying, 'These mountains have been dumb witnesses of struggles against Buddhism now only remembered by phrases about non-violence and non-attachment. Buddhism has been perfectly absorbed; India always does absorb each passing wave, making it her own in the eternal Samkhya Law,[2] Divine Nature, which is almighty power. Faces carved out of stone have been called successively, Shiva, Buddha, and again, Shiva. It has scarcely mattered. Some lips have always pronounced the Name of life itself.'

A door opened noiselessly and a young woman appeared, barefoot like myself, with her veil thrown back over her hair. I could not doubt that this girl with her bright eyes and shy smile was the wife of Panditji. 'Bahin,' she said, 'I do not speak very good English, but Panditji is teaching me. In the evening he sits beside me in our little garden and tells me the names of the stars and the flowers. I know all the words for talking about love, the children, and the rest of the family. It was I who got your luncheon ready today. Did you enjoy it? Who taught you to pick up your rice between your thumb and forefinger? I can show you a much better way. Are you coming to see us every day?'

---

[1] The *Veda:* any one of the four holy books of the Hindus.
[1] The Samkhya Law: A philosophy attributed to the Sage Kapila.

We were still standing when the Mother, a stout woman of about my own age, came into the room. The whole atmosphere changed. Our manners and gestures at once became formal. I bent to touch her feet, but she quickly came forward to touch mine. Then she took me by the hand and made me sit facing her on the carpet. Her daughter-in-law remained standing until the Mother pointed out a place for her, a little behind me and on my right. The Mother spoke nothing but Hindi, or Pahari, her native language, which is one of the highland dialects.

'What is your father's religion?' she asked me abruptly. 'I have read the Bible in Hindi. What interests me most is the angels. It does not always tell their names. Have you ever seen one?'

'When I was about four or five,' I answered, 'my grandmother gave me the picture of an angel dressed in pink. He was watching a little girl picking flowers beside a river.'

'Oh! I know that one,' she said, 'that is the guardian-angel, I know all about him! Do angels ever come and talk to you? What spiritual discipline do you follow?' she continued after a pause. 'Everybody has their own. Do you have a guru (a spiritual director)?'

'The guru who brought me to India,' I said, 'is the heroine of the book which I have been writing. But that is finished now!'

'Ah so your child is born! When a woman is pregnant, all she can think of is the child she bears. But, Bahin, that other embryo, your own Self, the one born of the spirit, do you feel that alive in you?'

'Indeed, I long to find a place for it, but what should I do? will you help me?'

'For more than forty years, I have been preparing a place for it myself, so that I may know its peace. It will come. But you need to be very religious and always watchful, for the body is full of fancies!'

At that precise moment, a child's piercing cries were heard coming from the garden, and Mother rose quickly and left the room. I heard her scolding, a man's voice, and the sound of a stick thrown on stones. 'My little boy is frightened of the buffaloes,' said Panditji's wife serenely. 'He will learn in time.'

When I left, I found Panditji going from rosebush to rosebush cutting off the dead heads, while behind him, a little servant-boy with a broom swept up the petals. 'Go quickly home,' he said, 'before it gets too hot. Your servant is waiting for you on the steps. Come again before you leave, I have some books that will interest you.'

I went back twice to Shanti Bhavan, but needed all my courage because, when you were not expected, the house was silent. On the first occasion I did not manage to make them hear and had to return home. Next time, I sent Singh to announce me and then, of course, Panditji was there to welcome me. The outer door was always open, it is true, but no one was ever in the rose garden and all the inner doors were kept shut. There was neither bell nor knocker, no sound came from the windows, although many people might have been looking through the tiny grilles. There was not even a dog. It was just like the palace of the Sleeping Beauty.

Yet all the time, I could feel that behind that forbidding wall there was an inner place full of busy women, playing children, and servants going backwards and forwards attending to their duties. Except on visiting days, there was no intercourse between this world and the one outside. How, I wondered, did they communicate?

When I went for the last time, to say good-bye to Panditji, he gave me a green coconut to pack among my luggage on my way to Calcutta, so that I might have the protection of the "Goddess of Happy Journeys". It was a particularly heavy nut and came from the goddess's own temple, where a woman is the official priestess and has sole responsibility.

When Christmas came three weeks later, I received a letter from Panditji with his good wishes and the following invitation. "If you are thinking of coming back to work in our highlands, next summer, I shall be glad if you will let me know as soon as possible. My house is yours, I should like you to stay here and think of it as your home. Shanti Bhavan is a very large house and quite ready to receive you, etc., etc."

I took this letter and showed it to the two advisers, who acted as my guides in Calcutta. One of them was a Swâmi, a monk belonging to a Vedantic religious brotherhood. He read the letter, looked severely at me, and said, 'This is quite out of the question,' and after a moment's pause, added, 'I shall make inquiries.' My other friend had been a barrister, and was a man of great experience who welcomed progressive ideas. But he, too, said, 'This would be impossible. For orthodox Brahmins to invite you to share a meal under special conditions is just conceivable, because the duties of hospitality are all-embracing. But if you were to live with them for any length of time you would create difficulties that would increase hourly. I cannot be more explicit. This invitation is a courtesy to a foreigner, a gesture to the outside world. The polite thing for you is to decline and then to wait.' I could drag nothing further from him.

A few days later, during which time letters might have been exchanged, the Swâmi gave me the following advice. 'Write to your friends expressing gratitude, but leave all the decisions to Pandit Vidyasagar's mother. Then think no more about it.'

That was easy enough for him to say. The Swâmi had his thoughts under control, but I was bubbling over with excitement in spite of the fact that I, too, was leading an extremely simple life, which the discipline of poverty had reduced to bare necessities. At that point tea was brought to us. As he was drinking, the Swâmi spoke again. 'Pandit Vidyasagar,' he

said, 'knows all about you. If the time has come for you to
"cross the threshold", that will happen. The system of yoga,
as practised in a Brahmin family like the one you are going to
visit, cannot be explained in books. It never obtrudes, yet it
is the very framework around our lives. It keeps each member
of the household in constant touch with the Rule that is so
strictly observed in the family hierarchy. That relationship is
continually strengthened by freely offered sacrifices, by means
of which life is perpetually renewed. It is the same vital energy
that brought the River Ganges down to earth from Heaven, a
miracle that is continually being repeated on every level of
consciousness.'

Obedient to the Swâmi's advice, I waited for three months.
It was April, and the hot weather had already begun, before I
received a second letter from Shanti Bhavan. "Bahin," it read,
"The little room that faces the outer court has been especially
whitewashed for you. Do not start on April 15th for that is a
most unlucky day. The great Agastya set forth on that day and
never returned. When you go North-west, take the evening
train on April 17th, and do not stop on the way."

When he had read the letter, the Swâmi said, 'You may go
now, but be careful to follow your instructions. Srî Râmakrishna[1] once sent Sârada Devî[2] all the way home after walking for many days, because she arrived at the temple of
Dakshineswar on an unlucky day. Take as little luggage as
possible.'

I did not expect him to say more, but he continued, 'You
have been living as a foreigner amid appalling poverty in the
Hindu quarter of Calcutta, dealing with problems of refugees,
kidnapped women, and abandoned children. Now you will feel

[1] Srî Râmakrishna (1836–86). Considered in India, to have been
a divine incarnation.
[2] Sârada Devî: The bride of the above. She lived in his native
village and sometimes paid long visits to the temple of Dakshineswar,
where he was priest.

a different kind of strangeness, new ideas, unfamiliar sensations, another way of life. It will be very quiet, but there will be compensations. Never ask questions, try not to act on impulse. Perhaps you may learn something new.'

I left, as arranged, by the evening train, on April 17th.

3

I Settle Into Shanti Bhavan

I SOON RAN INTO DIFFICULTIES THAT MIGHT EASILY HAVE made life impossible at Shanti Bhavan, but on my very first evening I already began to realize that I could cope with them if I were willing and able to adapt myself. Panditji had invited me; therefore he must have some part for me to play in the life of his household. It was for me to discover what that part was and I had much to learn. How should I begin?

I was sorely tempted to ask questions, but made a firm resolution, which, although I did not realize it at the time, demanded a tremendous amount of self-control. I determined never to ask "how?" or "why?" but to salute the unknown like a Hindu, with hands joined, for that, in itself, might prove to be the answer.

Contrary to my expectations, no one came to meet me when I arrived at Kurmachala by the evening omnibus. Since leaving Calcutta, I had been travelling for thirty-six hours by train and for ten by coach, and had been so much looking forward to seeing Panditji again that I felt disappointed, almost bewildered, when he was not among the excited horde of Nepalese coolies who fought over my luggage. I signed to them to stack my cases by the roadside and proceeded to sit down on my small tin trunk in order to take stock. Then, by gestures, I managed to order tea and wheaten cakes from a nearby covered stall. By that time, the bus-conductor had read the luggage labels and was loudly holding forth, as though he were familiar with my entire history.

At long last, a small boy with a runny nose and the smile of an angel appeared waving a crumpled note. "Bahin," I read, "Come straight up to the house. If you follow the servant, he will find coolies." The small boy then issued orders right and left, chose two men out of the crowd, struck a bargain with them for carrying my luggage, and, after he had lighted his lantern and put himself at the head of the procession, we set off.

As soon as we arrived at Shanti Bhavan, my guide showed me up a little spiral stairway to the gallery off which my room was situated. He also showed me a small hut at one end, containing a bucket of water, a cup for dipping into it, a mirror, and a *chaise-percée*. Then he disappeared. I felt overcome by the utter stillness and the vast expanse of the view from the gallery. The town of Kurmachala had been built upon a crest of the mountains. On one side steep ravines ran down to the River Koshi, on the other lay a deep valley, into which cropped spurs of the great snow-mountains, Trisul, Nanda Kot, Nanda Devî, and many others. Behind them I could imagine Tibet, very close as the bird flew, but twelve days march across the passes.

The coolies had brought up my luggage by this time. The room was so small and bare that it took little time to arrange my belongings, my blanket-roll upon the string bedstead and my papers upon the table. There was a padlocked door communicating with the interior of the house and two modern windows with glass panes, one of them overlooking the courtyard with the roses, and the other, to my intense joy, the inner court. I suddenly noticed, on the sill of the latter, a large flat stone sheltering some dried plants, sprigs of oats, and a few shreds of cloth. I was wondering how to open the window without disturbing the stone, when I sensed that someone had come silently into the room and was standing behind me watching—a cold, unfriendly presence.

It took me a moment or two to compose myself before I turned round and saw, bowing low before me, the family priest. He said that he had come to make sure that I was comfortable and to tell me that Panditji's eldest son, Anil, was about to visit me to ask me some questions. Then, pointing to the windowledge, he continued, 'That is a *yantra,* a talisman, from the Temple of Jageshwar, it must on no account be touched because a child's healing depends upon it. What is more, it must not be moved, otherwise we should have taken it away before you arrived.'

'May it prove an equally good omen for me', I said. 'You may be sure that I shall not disturb it,' and I also bowed deeply. The priest then left the room as silently as he had come, so lightly, indeed, and so softly that he seemed to dissolve into thin air. He had spoken perfect English, with an Oxford accent. About twenty minutes later Anil appeared, a powerfully built boy of about fifteen years old. He was so nervous that he stammered, saying that he preferred to remain standing when I asked him to sit down, but when I myself sat on the edge of the bed, he consented to sit on the floor, at a lower level as a sign of respect. 'I bring you greetings from my grandmother and my mother,' he at last managed to say in very broken English. 'My grandmother wishes to know how she should prepare your meals. Of course Naraïn could bring them here. He says that he wipes the dust from your feet and would be proud to wait on you. But if you would prefer to eat downstairs before we do, my father would eat with you.'

Thus, I found myself immediately confronted with a most delicate decision before even I had set eyes on Panditji, and with no one to advise me. I knew that in orthodox Brahmin families the question of food was a matter of the strictest taboo, and I was aware that upon my answer would depend the terms on which I should stand with each separate member of the family so long as I remained in their house. On the one hand I risked exclusion, but on the other, Naraïn, the Brahmin, was accepting me as a superior. There followed a long silence during which I tried to make my face a blank, hoping that Anil would think that I was choosing words which he would understand. In reality, I was composing an answer that would relieve me of the decision by handing it back to the family. Finally, I said, 'Anil, your grandmother follows her own rule of life, I wish to follow mine. Will you ask her to decide?' Anil repeated my sentence several times to make sure of the exact wording and then ran quickly away so as to have no chance of forgetting.

I scarcely had time to wonder what would happen next, before Naraïn appeared, looking pleased, carrying in one hand a tray of food, and in the other, a jug of drinking water. He spoke no English, merely adding to his very much Sanskritized Hindi the kind of gestures that would help me to understand him. 'Here,' he said, 'are vegetables, sweet peppers, cream custard, and hard corn-cakes. Mataji has cooked them. Tomorrow morning at ten, I shall bring your rice-meal. Here is also milk. We have three cow-buffaloes that never leave our paddock.' He carried the little table to the bed on which I was sitting, placed the tray, which was also my plate, upon it, and switched on the electric light. He went into ecstasies as the light appeared, telling me that electricity was quite new in Kurmachala and very expensive, whereas, he said, according to the Vedas, the prophets had used it thousands of years ago, when they wished to make water gush out of the ground, dress monolithic stones, or set light to sacrifices with their wands. He stood watching me eat, having said on my behalf the ritual words that accompany the first five mouthfuls of rice. When I had finished he called a servant-boy of about fifteen years old, who swept the floor scrupulously clean of crumbs.

'We must not tempt the wild-cats, rats, or ants,' he said. 'They do not waste their time when there is nothing to steal.'

It was nine o'clock on that first evening before Panditji came to see me, climbing quickly up my little staircase and filling the doorway with his tall figure. He cast an anxious glance round the room, obviously searching for something, until his eye came to rest upon my typewriter, when I noticed the same approving look that I had seen earlier in Naraïm. My blessed "Baby Hermes" was my warrant, just as a stethoscope hanging carelessly from a pocket proclaims the doctor, a man who knows the answers, speaks English, and cures fevers. Panditji then unlocked the door leading into the next room from which he fetched a chair, placing it in front of my table, and making me sit on it to assure himself that I could work comfortably. He informed me that his three servants were at my disposal and that one of them would take my letters to the post and accompany me to the town if I wished to go out. I also learned that a low-caste woman had been engaged to empty my pail and bring fresh water, and that she would be my personal responsibility. I was to pay her a rupee and a half every week. Not a word was said about my journey but I could see that he was fully informed of all that I had done, said, and eaten.

When he joined the tips of his fingers to say good-bye, he made the unusual remark, 'Have I your permission to withdraw?' because I had forgotten the little nod which automatically brings conversations to an end. Even after two years spent in India I still found it hard to dismiss visitors, which was why I rather stupidly added, 'Will you please thank your mother for me and give her my respects?' Panditji stared at me. 'Why do you say that,' he asked, 'I am always reading that phrase in English novels, and one hears it said in government offices. Does offering your respect to my mother mean that you wish to live as she lives. That is how we should interpret the remark in India. I shall tell her so.'

Panditji then left me, and I began to undo my sarî, before going to bed. From the kitchen I could hear the noise of running water and pots and pans being dried. In the distance, there were other noises, the chirping of frogs and crickets and that rustling of the wind in bushes, that makes one think of rain. Suddenly the curtain across the doorway was lifted and Panditji's wife, dressed in a plain cotton sarî, came into the room.

'I am to come every evening,' she said. 'Panditji says that I am to talk to you; but what about? I am so ignorant. My whole life is spent in this house.' I sat down beside her and asked her the age of her youngest baby.

'Fourteen months.'

'Will you lend him to me sometimes? What is his name?'

'We call him "Ganthu"; it means a little bell. He is always laughing.'

She was so shy and I so tired after my long journey that I did not feel able to make the slightest effort, not even that of being nice to her. Instead, I took my pillow in my arms and began to rock it like a baby, singing,

> *'Sleep my little one, sleep in the mist,*
> *'The sheep they bleat in the fold . . .*

As I sang the last notes of my lullaby, it was the head of my new friend that I held against my breast, and her forehead that my fingers were stroking.

Panditji's Uncles

Well before five o'clock on the following morn-
ing, I was wakened by discordant cries. At first, I thought that
people were shrieking for help, but when the shrill voices
suddenly ceased, and then began to take up the same cries in
unison, I flew to the window to see where these high-pitched,
disjointed prayers could be coming from. On the stone roof of
one of the houses below, two Brahmins were sitting, bawling
at the tops of their voices. They sat as upright as the letter "I",
their eyes open, their faces turned towards the sun. Their
whole bodies shook with the effort of their holy chanting of
the *Surya Namaskar*, the Salute to the Sun. From one of the
other houses came the booming of a conch-shell, that extraordinary moaning sound which is sent out from before the
altar towards the four points of the compass during the morning service. Everywhere bells were being rung with the greatest energy.

Shanti Bhavan was still asleep. The very first sound was of
a door banging in the courtyard. The servants were beginning
to go about their business, some to light the braziers with
great sweeps of their fans, which made the smoke swirl upwards, others to carry pitchers to the water tank. Curious-
looking figures they appeared, with their legs and the lower

part of their bodies bare and their shoulders covered with voluminous woollen shawls. Several other men in a corner of the yard were gargling, snorting, cleaning their tongues, splashing themselves with water and pouring it over their heads. I noticed Panditji among them and wondered whether they all lived in the house and whether each one had a wife and children.

Then the house began humming like a hive of bees. A chant was droned out on a hurdy-gurdy, and I could hear the rhythmical beat of Sanskrit phrases, repeated with long hissing sounds, followed by silences and pauses for prostration. All Shanti Bhavan was praying, except Mother whom I saw crossing the court, her veil over her head and in her hands a bunch of flowers and a copper water-jug. I opened both sides of my double door and drew back the hanging curtain, emblem of the movable frontier between myself and the other occupants of the house, between a foreign woman and the inner life of the family.

When Naraïn appeared with a glass of very hot, strong, sweet tea mixed with whey, he found me already seated at my typewriter, with a piece of carbon paper in my hand and an open dictionary beside me. I had been feeling a little lonely in a rhythm to which I was not yet attuned and, as always, I had taken refuge in writing up the notes of my journeys, the last of which had been from Calcutta to Kurmachala. But I was given little time for writing.

My visitors, that first morning, were the uncles of Panditji. They came one after the other with great solemnity to greet the house-guest, the strange woman whom their nephew was bringing into the family circle. The first uncle lived in the room next mine. He was a clever-looking, talkative man, whose conversation was chiefly about himself. He told me that he was a high-official in the post-office, and that he was paying a long visit to his nephew while convalescing from a severe attack of anaemia, which had developed suddenly. As soon as he was fit to travel, without giving any warning, he, his wife, his two sons, and a servant, had set out for Shanti Bhavan, by his doctor's advice.

He asked me whether I should like to meet his sons, who were, he said, the apples of his eye and the repose of his declining years. 'The future of my line is assured,' he continued, 'I have fulfilled my duty to society. Even if one of my sons were to die, the other would be there to inscribe our name in the family tree (*gotra*). The current must not cease to flow, for that would be a crime against life. Think how waves are born out of the curve of their own recession. It was my duty to follow their example.'

He leaned out of the window and shouted. I heard footsteps scampering up the staircase and there appeared four boys of approximately the same age, which might have been anything from nine to eleven. The uncle said, 'These are the young sons of the family. They are really what you would call two pairs of cousins, but they do not think so, they feel like brothers. Only their mothers are different, their fathers are of the same stock.'

I must have shown surprise at such small children having so elderly a father, for he said, 'They were born after I had been married for thirty years. Yes, it was a stern test for me, and many times I was tempted to take a second wife so as to safeguard my line. All my family urged me to do so, but at last God took pity on us, for it would have broken my wife's heart. We made together all the pilgrimages prescribed for those who wish for children, we visited the proper temples and gave offerings to the gods and priests, but all in vain, until one day we heard of a foreign woman who, like you, had spent a long time in an ashram. She, also, respected our ways of thought, philosophy and beliefs and, like you again, she was a doctor. My wife had never before consulted one, but she let herself be treated and when an operation was considered necessary she had it, and it cost me fifty rupees—at that time a great deal of money, but I paid it gladly. My eldest son was born just ten months afterwards, and the younger a year later.'

He stopped talking and touched the children's heads. 'On the day when my second son was born,' he continued, 'my wife and I made a vow of chastity, and another to devote our lives to the service of the Temple of Purî after our sons' marriages, which will be in five or six years' time.'

'I am very much moved by what you say,' I answered, 'but I ought to tell you that I am not a doctor.'

'You cannot alter facts,' said the uncle, looking at my hands. 'You may not have studied medicine, but yours are hands that know how to touch the aching spot and relax strained nerves. I shall tell my wife to come and see you; she will teach you massage, how to smooth away fatigue and nervous twitchings, and still the passions, like anger and fear, that do violence to our muscles. . . .'

It was Naraïn who announced the arrival of the second uncle. I saw before me a jolly-looking, rather stout man with a very light complexion, who sat upon a mat spread on the floor, facing him. He paid me not the slightest attention, but seemed literally to be imbibing the atmosphere of my room until, suddenly, his eye lit on the *Bhagavad-Gîtâ*[1] lying among my papers, with a Sanskrit alphabet of movable letters, like the ones used for teaching children to read.

'Good gracious!' he said in great surprise. 'The Gîtâ! Do you know the twelfth chapter by heart?'

'No, I know the substance of it quite well, but I do not know it in your sense of the word.'

Instead of answering, he began to recite the whole chapter aloud, chanting the end of each verse in a minor key. I recognized the lines as he said them and was able to join him in

---

[1] That most sacred of all books, also called the *Song of the Blessed*, forms part of the *Mahâbhârata,* a long historical and mystical poem.

repeating the words of the final salutation, which is accompanied by an inclination of the head. He then proceeded to embark upon a feat of memory of which I had often heard. He recited the whole chapter backwards.

When he had finished he said with a charming smile, 'It is delightful to feel, even for a moment, that one is the vehicle by which the first and the last words of the text are linked together, and by which the last is again linked to the first. One feels like the string of a necklace when all the beads are properly threaded. The string knows nothing of the thought underlying the words, nor has it intelligence to understand the text, but nevertheless, it exists. It is the humble tool by means of which the spirit of the words is brought to us. Without the string there would be no necklace.'

I was making an effort to understand what he was saying, and he must have seen it from my expression, for he suddenly stopped. 'No!' he said, 'do not try to think! If you do, you will accuse me of being pedantic, whereas I only meant to explain that one can get the feeling of the words as they uncoil and recoil, a sensation that is pure in itself. When Bramah created the universe, the conceptual power proceeded exactly like the numbers, 1, 2, 3, 4, 5, etc.; but when Shiva destroys the universe, the last created will be the first to go and the numbers will retrogress, 5, 4, 3, 2, 1. The secret of finding the moment of perfection—you are a Christian, you would probably call it "Grace"—is to recognize the point "x", at which the rhythm changes direction.'

He ceased speaking, made a vague gesture and went on, 'Makesh came to see you earlier this morning. He probably spoke to you of the wave being born in its own recession. That is the bee in his particular bonnet. Mine is to explain the same idea by the symbol "x", which stands both for the starting-point and the goal. You see, I am a mathematician. Everybody has a different feeling about the same thing. You, too, when you have ceased trying to discover meaning by adding one word to another, will have that wonderful sensation of "being", instead of knowing. The only way to understand this kind of thing is through ideas. . . .'

After a long silence, he began to speak on a different subject. 'Panditji tells me that when you talk together there is real communication. If only that could be true! That is why he invited you to Shanti Bhavan. I, myself, was against the idea for several weeks.'

'I am glad that you have told me. I should probably have felt he same had I been you. After all, I am a foreigner, and I know how intolerant many of our clergy are towards the Hindu religion. May I ask you one question?', I continued. 'Why did you invite me? Why give this opportunity to me, in particular?' Immediately, I sensed that I had been premature, and quickly added, 'Will you please go on telling me about Chapter 12; the one which you have been reciting.'

'Not today,' he said, 'but I will sometimes pay you a morning visit, and we will continue the conversation.'

The third uncle was impeccably dressed in a lounge-suit, tailored in the English fashion from a woollen cloth, called *khaddar,* which is woven in the villages. He looked a man of the world, urbane, sensitive, exceedingly distinguished, and was wearing the white forage-cap of the followers of Ghandi. He had more than nine years of imprisonment to his credit. After India had gained her independence, his political career had obliged him to spend a large part of the year in Delhi. I thought him more approachable than the two other uncles, as though he were carrying on a conversation with an invisible presence at the same time as he was talking to me. It was he who asked me some of the questions that I had been expecting.

'Who gave you the money to come so far?'

'If your husband, why is he not with you?'

'Where does he live? How does he earn a living?'

'Where did you land in India, and where did you spend your first night?'

'Are your parents still alive?'

'Have you any children?'

'Are you one of those many foreign women who wish to adopt a system of yoga, or are in search of a guru?'

His dictatorial manner made me answer him in sentences as clipped as his own, and just as impersonal. I determined to play his game. On another day, it would be my turn to ask him similar questions. I did not then realize that this conversation was leading us straight to essentials and making us friends.

He ended by saying, 'Panditji tells us you are seeking a Rule of life. Our discipline has existed since the world began, perhaps that is where you may find your own, if you can succeed in detaching it from its formal ritual. Although you may think differently now, try to accept the fact that there is no merging of religions in India, all are separate. It will help you if you remember that. This explanation, however, is only true on the intellectual plane, in practice, all the spokes of the "wheel of the *dharma*" (the Law) converge towards the centre. On that sublime level, everything is a matter of personal experience, of little miracles.

'But there is something else that I want to say. Now that you are here, I am glad. I am wondering how long you will be able to live among us without asking for explanations, instead of searching for equivalents in your own life. The western women, whom I meet in Delhi, are always asking "Why?" But there is no why. What is more, our own women, those who are students, are also beginning to ask "Why?" and we do not know how to answer them. The earth asks no questions of the wind. She captures it as it blows, nurses the seeds which it brings, and when those seeds grow into trees and grass, she infuses them with her own spirit. That is the whole secret.'

There was no answer to that. I felt as though I were standing at the foot of an immensely high wall, yet sure that I should eventually discover how to climb it. As in the Hindu parable, I had to find the silken thread which the beetle clutched as he crept along the side and finally reached the top. The uncle was gazing straight out into the distance with the far-away look of the prisoner whom he once had been, when the silence was unfortunately interrupted by the arrival of a man of about forty years old. 'Ah!' he exclaimed. 'Here is my nephew Ashok, he is a barrister with a practice in this town. I think I shall appoint him your *cavaliere servente.*'

Then, without raising his head, he issued a series of orders in Hindi, to which the new-comer listened, standing. The uncle then turned to me and said, 'I have told him to take you for walks, show you the school, help you when you go shopping, introduce our cousins, take you to the Temple, and answer any questions that you like to ask.'

He indicated a place where Ashok might sit, and the two men began to speak of their own affairs in their native dialect, paying no further attention to me. In the twinkling of an eye I had become a background to their talk, a piece of scenery, a woman, present but silent, an indispensable element of passive consciousness. At that precise moment when I was of so little concern to them, I began to feel that I had my place in their family.

When the uncle had gone, Ashok stayed long enough for me to ask what it was that his uncle feared for me. He hesitated a moment and then said, 'You will learn that the lives of all of us here have a particular significance because they depend on the self-sacrifice of two women. One of them is the mother of Panditji, and the other is my aunt. Panditji's mother you will certainly know because it was she who invited you here, but you will never see my aunt because she receives no one. Throughout my uncle's imprisonment she lived in absolute seclusion with her father and the children, who were very small at that time. It was because of her self-sacrifice and strict self-discipline that my uncle found strength to endure. Because these two women make so complete a sacrifice the life of this family is given proper direction. Try to remem-

ber, when you get up in the morning and lie down to sleep at
night, that these two women are awake and watching over us.'

'What do their lives consist of?'

Ashok smiled, 'Say, rather, what do they not consist of?'

That same evening, the uncle who had spoken of the Gîtâ,
came to see me again. When he lifted the curtain with one
hand and came in, he found me lying upon the bed. I was re-
living the conversations of the morning and trying, as it were,
to think behind the spoken words so as to understand the
meaning of what Ashok and the uncles had been telling me. I
realized that all depended on me whether or not I became intimate with these friends, for I was enfolded by their goodwill,
yet all day long I had been conscious of a feeling of depression.
Our lives seemed to lie parallel. Should I ever develop enough
tact, understanding and wisdom to bring them together and
enter simply and naturally into the family? Should I be capable
of putting myself into a state of mind to learn everything from
the beginning, to live and laugh and think like a little child,
yet still bear in mind the values of my own kind of civilization? It would mean abandoning my own tempo of life and
conforming to theirs. This I understood and was ready to do,
but should I ever succeed? Only by living in their home as
part of their family could I hope to discover that which is the
One Abiding Truth.

I had no need to speak, for the uncle knew at once what
was tiring me. He bent over my typewriter and said, 'How
much have you written today?'

'Nothing.'

'Why not?'

'I have been trying to think about what we were saying this
morning and I find that I cannot understand.'

He simply laughed. 'If you persist in trying to understand
by thinking you will never succeed, for there are no lessons to
be learned by heart and no homework to prepare for the next
day. It is as though you had set in motion a whole series of

wheels in a piece of machinery which you have not yet
learned to control. If you think about it you will meet difficulty after difficulty, whereas, in fact, it is very simple. When
I speak to you, you are my thought, when you speak to me, I
am yours, because we are, as it were, under the same roof.
Now that you are one of us, your old life will seem a series of
past experiences that will help you in reaching out to something new and strange. You do not yet know what that something is, but you must be ready to receive it. Be like the eagle
when it spreads its wings and plunges down into the abyss.
The eagle does not think about flying, it simply feels that it
flies.'

He left me, and I felt literally overcome by a totally unexpected feeling of nervousness.

5

The Ancestor

PANDITJI'S WIFE CONTINUED TO VISIT ME EVERY evening in my room, but she came purely out of courtesy to a distinguished guest. I knew in advance all that she would say in her inscrutably gentle manner, with exquisite gestures and the smile of the miniatures upon her lips. Should we ever break down this barrier of formality? Time was passing, and very soon it would be three weeks since my arrival.

I knew from Anil that the family were in a state of grave anxiety because Panditji's great-uncle, the youngest brother of his grandfather, had an attack of fever and could see no one. He was a very old gentleman of over eighty, and was so deeply respected that his name was never uttered. He was known as "Maharaj", which means "great rajah", or "most noble lord". I had already realized that until Maharaj accepted me I should never become intimate with the women of the family.

During the days that followed I went for long walks with Ashok in order to know the country, and gradually became used to having my meals in quarantine, as it were. My idea that they all sat down, as we do, to a family meal from which I was excluded, turned out to be quite wrong. Everyone ate as and when it suited them before they went out to work in the morning. By looking out of my window, which gave me an excellent view of the inner court, I had begun to know the comings and goings of the various members of the family.

The morning began from the time when Mataji made her way to the kitchen. Everyone had their special task; Naraïn, for instance, had already told me that it was his duty to boil the rice in a special earthenware pan on a fire built for that purpose. Each month, on a certain day of the lunar calendar, the pan was broken as a hygienic precaution and replaced by a new one. One day I happened to see the servants crushing up the broken fragments before scattering them over the garden path.

Naraïn also peeled the vegetables and ground up the spices between two round stones, while Mataji attended to the cooking and two little kitchen-boys kneaded the dough for the *chupatties,* thin cakes of unleavened bread, which were brought to my room all crisp and still covered with ashes.

My tray was the first to be brought up. The two children ate their principal meal before going to school, and the men, whenever they felt hungry or their engagements allowed, for many of them were judges, magistrates, barristers, or attorneys attached to the Law Courts. I used to see them removing their sandals in the yard and washing their feet and hands at a tap provided for that purpose, before they sat down with their backs to the wall under the projecting eaves of the kitchen. Copper trays and bowls shone before them in the sunshine, and Naraïn waited upon them attentively, with most scrupulous care. They ate rapidly, without talking, for all were eager to go back to their business until the evening.

When they had gone, three old women used to appear, who took a long time over their meal. They sat in a circle and gossiped. I could hear them laughing like children, and when at length they finished, they stretched their thin legs out into the sun and expertly savoured a quid of betel-nut. They visibly relaxed, like cats in the warmth. I never managed to see their faces, because they kept one hand upon their veils, ready to adjust them if they slipped. Naraïn told me that they were the family-widows and ate only once a day. On fast-days, the eleventh of each lunar month, when we were eating puffed rice, various kinds of milky foods, and sugar cane, they had nothing at all, and they ate nothing on Mondays, which were devoted to the worship of the Divine Mother. Thus, when the eleventh happened to fall on either a Sunday or a Tuesday, they fasted completely for forty-eight hours. 'They are far ahead of us,' said Naraïn, 'for we find it hard to control our appetites. They are always laughing because they have nothing left to desire.'

'And Mataji——?' I began, but broke off quickly, fearing that I might become indiscreet.

'Mataji always eats alone, after the rest have done,' said Naraïn in a different tone. 'She cooks her own food. She is not like anyone else.'

Early one morning before seven o'clock, Anil called up to me from the garden. 'Bahin, Panditji is going down to Ananda Bhavan to see our great-uncle. He wants to know whether you would like to go with him. He leaves at once.' But before I had time to run out on to the terrace, Panditji entered my room. 'Come quickly,' he said, 'it is a perfect moment.'

I was still wearing the sarî in which I had been sleeping, and it was all in creases. I was just about to ask for three minutes to change into a fresh one, when Panditji began scolding. 'Come exactly as you are! Be your natural self! Where is your true womanhood? Whenever I see you, you are always far too well groomed, your sarî is always freshly ironed; you look like a picture. Here you are at home, not on ceremony. You should be your real self—or are you only a hot-house fruit?'

Coming my hair as I went, I followed Panditji down the stairs and along a shortcut, a path intersected by high stone steps, which ran across one end of the garden. He himself was dressed rather oddly, in a sleeveless green pull-over over a loose shirt, and with a *dhoti* round his waist. His head was muffled in a thick scarf, but his lower half was most scantily covered.

It seemed to me positively grotesque to go off at that time of the morning in such very informal clothes to pay a call on the most important member of the family. But I had many more surprises to come.

Panditji's head was still full of the idea that I resembled a fruit. He stopped for a moment to point out the terraced orchards on the slopes of the neighbouring hills. 'See!', he said, 'the English planted most of those orchards with the wild apricots that have given their name to the entire district—the Kumaon Hills. The forest-bushes originally produced a sour fruit with a large stone, but the flesh was a cure for most of the local sicknesses. By scientific methods, the English have completely altered the character of the plant. They have pruned and treated the roots and thus given new form to the branches. But can you imagine how violently the balance of the whole plant has been upset by this treatment? Nevertheless, after pruning, cutting and grafting, the new trees now produce apricots as large as ducks' eggs. Two of our cousins went to study this branch of science at an agricultural college. They have now returned with their diplomas as agricultural experts.'

When we reached Ananda Bhavan, a young servant was waiting to announce us, an unattractive, barefooted child, dressed up in an English shirt at least three sizes too big for him. He showed us into a room that ran the entire length of the building. In its centre, upon a square-shaped bed, the Ancestor sat cross-legged upon a tigerskin. His back was erect and he held his head high. He wore the saffron-coloured robe of Vedantic monks, and the great rosary with 108 beads of Shivite ascetics. A tin box and a few blue exercise books, lying on the thin cotton mattress, appeared to represent the whole sum of his worldly possessions.

I followed Panditji closely, and when he prostrated himself I bowed very low indeed, uttering the word *"pranam"*, that reverent and most tender of greetings, wherein the individuality is entirely obliterated, and those in harmony discover that they are spiritually akin. It was, however, such a tremendous shock to find myself thus abruptly brought face to face with a yogi[1] that I felt my eyes fill with tears and foolishly tried to hide my embarrassment by covering my face with my right hand. At the same time, I was thoroughly ashamed of myself for being so little mistress of the situation.

Could it be possible, I thought, that these families contained men of an older generation, like Maharaj, who had travelled far along the way of self-denial and yet remained full of human kindness? I felt his gentle eyes search mine and saw that he knew in a flash why my heart was troubled. I could not speak. Why had Panditji not warned me that Maharaj was a holy man?

The servant-boy now brought two bowls of tea for Panditji and myself, and fruit, peeled and cut into small pieces. Using Panditji as interpreter, the Ancestor wished me a happy time in his nephew's house, where, he said, a wedding was about to be celebrated. It was a marriage by which he set great store, not for himself, he added, but because the bridegroom and bride had been selected with great care, and high hopes were aroused by their union.

By this time, the news of our arrival must have spread, for while he was speaking, several other relatives or neighbours had come into the room and were sitting or standing behind us in order of rank or age. I began to realize that all manner of questions were being asked about me and that Panditji was giving replies, telling of my family and education, my past experiences, my travels, and what I had been doing in India. He was describing the way in which I lived, ate, thought, and reacted, for all the world as though I was a child of ten incapable of answering for myself, and he was making a report to some superior. I felt that the situation was totally alien to

[1] An ascetic who follows a rule of life.

me. All my pride melted away, as I became conscious that I really had no power to act on my own behalf. What did I represent for these people? What was I doing among them? The life of self-sacrifice led by the aged uncle moved me deeply. It seemed like clear crystal, in which one was mirrored as plainly as in a looking-glass. If I should try to see myself in the same way, what would happen? I discovered that, until then, I had never dared to look at myself objectively, or examine myself as these people were examining me. They seemed neutral, yet at the same time they must have felt kindly disposed, or they would not have admitted me into their homes. When I rose to take my leave, I felt so much disturbed that my knees would scarcely support me.

Panditji and I returned by a different and much longer way and without speaking. I needed quiet, for something within me was protesting against what had been happening, although the others seemed to have thought it natural enough.

Shortly before we reached Shanti Bhavan, a little procession passed, consisting of three turbaned policemen carrying rifles, at the head of a dozen convicts linked together with iron chains attached to their feet and hands. They walked leisurely, two by two, to the accompaniment of clanking iron. Three other policemen brought up the rear. It was a scene from the Middle Ages, chains, rags, and cudgels, only here, the police seemed the more uncomfortable. The prisoners were returning from interrogation at the law courts.

'The gaol in the Fort is not too bad,' said Panditji. 'I spent a long time there, long enough to write a book. Jahawal Nehru had the cell next to mine and my cousin was opposite. In the winter they used to take us down to the plains. Of course, the offences committed by these prisoners are very different from ours; conditions of life vary, and so do people's responsibilities. Every crime is related to the way in which people deal with their circumstances. One should never judge nor condemn, because there is always some factor unknown.'

'But, Panditji, you yourself are a judge!'

'Yes, for the moment, because that happens to be my job. I have a wife and children to bring up. I must provide for their comfort and give them every chance; that is my duty as head of the family and I do the best I can for them. I also owe a duty to Society, but such laws were laid down by men, and they are false doctrine. I obey them in small things because they serve to keep order in small matters. In big things I withhold judgment, because more than the crime and the culprit have to be considered; both exist, of course, but in a relationship which is necessary to evolution. The Law varies on every level of consciousness, and so do our obligations, duties, and perceptions of the proper thing to do. For instance, at this present moment, the right thing for me is to help you to gain a new vision of your surroundings. What will you make of it all? I wonder! Life is going to be much harder for you in the future, but it will have a different meaning. When you go back to your own country, you will have to reconstitute your values before you can feel at home with your own people. It may take you two, or even three years; who knows? Very few people indeed have had your opportunities in one lifetime,' he added after a moment's thought.

Panditji had sat down upon a little knoll, from which, through a gap in the hills, one could see the white peak of Kedarnath, one of the Holy Mountains of the Himalayas, to which thousands of pilgrims climb each year. 'It is like returning from up there,' said Panditji. 'You never come back as you go, even although you may not at first realize it. It changes one drastically to meet oneself face to face, literally to feel the presence of God, to hear in one's heart the voice of *Him who sits between the Worlds,* to know the absolute purity of that which has neither name nor form. Later comes sure knowledge that the Self is a mosaic of many-coloured stones, each having its separate urge. All these different selves are the tattered rags to which we have grown accustomed. How comfortable they are! How well they conceal the True Self, which is far too shy to appear! Yet that same Self was the one with which Râmakrishna writhed in ecstacy, and with Self he saw the Divine Mother go out on to the roof of the Temple of Dakshineswar. He followed Her! He spoke to Her!'

Then, dreamily, Panditji began to recite:

> *To the Ganges She turns Her face,*
> *Her dark hair floats in the wind,*
> *On Her feet the anklets tinkle,*
> *She is the call of the sea*
> *The gale dies on Her breath.'*

Panditji rose. 'You must discard many shapes and forms before you are able to see Her,' he said, 'and your body's eyes will not avail.' Then he added almost angrily as he turned to face me, 'Are you still thinking about your silk sarî, which you said was so important, this morning.'

6

Questions

$\mathcal{A}$SHOK CAME TO SEE ME THAT SAME EVENING.

'Ashok,' I said, 'why did you not warn me that Maharaj was a *sannyasin*,[1] a mendicant, who has renounced the world?'

'Because you never inquired,' he said at length. 'The great Manu[2] bids us answer all questions, but you did not ask any. And then, you had only learned from books about the possibilities of renunciation as a means of perfecting a full and active life. What use in speaking before the time was ripe?'

'How can you know what is going to be new to me?'

'Your gestures are very revealing, and your face is expressive. You could never tell a lie, except in words, for no one has taught you the technique of self-control, whereas we have made an exact science of it.'

'Does that make you any happier?'

'That is not the question. We may, perhaps, be more conscious of the place which each one of us occupies in the universe. But how strange you are! You take your emotions so seriously and you allow them to ruffle the waters of your spirit. Yet there is no direct connection. There is simply the interplay of the real and the illusory—but that you cannot see.'

[1] One who has taken the supreme vows of obedience, chastity, and poverty.
[2] The great lawgiver of the tenth century B.C., the supposed author of the Mânavadharmashâstra.

'Indeed, I do realize that something is wrong, although I cannot understand what it is. I felt it very much this morning, when those people criticized me to my face, and made a kind of inventory of my possibilities and limitations.'

'But why should they not? If you once accept the fact that these people want to help you to self-knowledge, you will learn many things about yourself which you do not already know. We cannot change the outline of our lives, nor our outward circumstances, but inwardly, as a musician plays upon his instrument, we can select from hour to hour our particular rhythm and mode of expression. There are rhythms to suit each different thought. That is what you do not yet understand, and that is where the observation of others may help you.'

By this time I was beginning to feel uncomfortable, as Ashok quickly realized. 'This is all quite stupid,' he said, 'and it is all my fault. I believed that you had already sensed all this, but as yet, you only know it with your mind.'

I could not answer, and feeling a little vexed at my reaction I led him out on to the terrace. I knew that I could not do without him, I needed his help to climb this obstacle which I had discovered in my path, but I found his direct, slightly ironical manner and his evident patience most irritating. He came back to the subject, however, and tried to explain. 'Even I,' he said, 'do not know what I am, except through my relationships with others. Some are higher on the ladder than I, and some are below me. Panditji, for example, is senior to me, but for Anil, I am the elder and can do no wrong. He asks me anything that comes into his head, and thus I am partly responsible for any doubts which he may feel. May his knowledge of the evil in life not come to him from any actions of mine!'

Ashok, as I fully realized, was showing me that I had my place, albeit a very low one, in the chain of family responsibilities, which meant that I should give some proof of my willingness to obey. But obey what? A Rule which I still could not name, and of which I could still only grasp the most elementary principles? Must I accept that compared with Panditji and the uncles I was totally ignorant, and that as regards the children, I must assume responsibility? That, indeed, was the whole matter, and in the days that followed Ashok explained everything in great detail. It became the subject of most of our conversations. 'The acharya will always help you when the threads get tangled,' he said, 'life is just like trying to find one's way through the jungle.'

Once again I asked him the question that was chiefly occupying my mind. 'How did Maharaj become a sannyasin?'

Ashok then told me the following story, which I wrote down that same evening; but what most impressed me was his posture as he spoke of Maharaj. He sat up very straight, his breathing quietened, and his voice became gentle, as though he were talking of a little child. It was quite obvious that Maharaj's life expressed Ashok's own ideal, his deepest longing, which nothing else would satisfy. For every member of the family, Maharaj represented the Rule, as it should be lived upon the human plane, without compromise, display, or limitations. No, Ashok said, he was not a Holy Man, nor a Freed-Soul, nor even a man who had achieved the Supreme Aim. Such things could not be expressed in words, for how could one establish degrees of holiness. 'What do such words mean now that foreigners have taken them into everyday speech,' said Ashok sadly. 'The West has discovered that we have a living religion, and they talk as glibly of *asana, samâdhi,* and liberation, as fifty years ago they discussed the virtues of tea and pepper. India is the fashion now. Should we fear to export our philosophies and our swâmis, since you send us your gospels and your missionaries? Perhaps these two methods of penetration may be complementary, and produce the fermentation necessary to evolution.'

Ashok was careful not to hurt my feelings, but at the same

time he was determined that I should think of Maharaj's life as though it were something fixed, like a photograph. 'It is the crowning of a long, hard, and active life,' he said, 'and it still continues to be hard and active upon a different plane. Although Maharaj appears so passive, he is the centre to which several generations gravitate. Ganthu, the baby, has already learned to bow to him. Anil, the adolescent, does the same, and the men of our family prostrate themselves and touch his feet with their foreheads.'

Maharaj did not often speak, he added, but when he did, it was always with the wisdom of experience. Every problem brought to him he saw by the light of the undeniable truth, and in his presence no one was either right or wrong, but each one discovered what he was in his True Self and what he should do in his difficulties.

'Even with Maharaj's help,' continued Ashok, 'there is a long road to travel before one can find the solution to one's problems. First, one has to learn many things and learn to understand them well, and then, one day, one realizes that the hardest thing of all is to forget everything before one begins to act. At that point, whatever remains in one's heart is one's own, because it has been sublimated. This is true humility, for everything that has name and form must eventually vanish away in order that the underlying truth may arise and be made manifest. I still have a long way to go, I may never arrive, but even to understand these things is a great step forwards.'

Maharaj's life story turned out to be a very simple one. Twenty years earlier he had had a serious illness, which the doctors of Allahabad had warned him would be his last. He had returned home and had spent an entire winter in settling his affairs, for there was a question of property-boundaries, and the marriage of a niece to be arranged. His health grew steadily worse, but he went on with the work systematically, and when all was accomplished, he summoned his family to tell them of his decision to renounce the world and live face to face with the Lord, continually repeating His Holy Name. All of which was so much in conformity with tradition that none of his relatives attempted to dissuade him.

He then discarded his Brahmin cord, the badge of his caste, and put on the saffron robe of a monk. For three days he remained at home, speaking to no one, but blessing little children when they were brought to him, and eating nothing but rice, milk-foods, and fruit. Then, one evening, he left, taking with him nothing at all.

For five years, during which time he may have entered an ashram, they lost all trace of him and gave him up for dead, until, one day, they heard that he was living at a mountain-temple a few miles from the town. His eldest son sent him word through a priest that if he chose to return to his old home he would be given the impersonal welcome due to an itinerant monk. 'Later, perhaps,' came the reply from the sannyasin.

So the great room at Ananda Bhavan was given a fresh coat of lime-wash, but ten years passed before the old man returned, and by that time, his son had been dead for two years.

Maharaj now lived in solitude. He saw his family only in the morning, very early, and only on certain days during the week.

7

Troubles

I HAD BEEN WAKING UP FEELING UNHAPPY FOR SEVeral days past. My life was like looking at some beautiful painting in which I could see many fascinating people, but had no means of communicating with them. I tried in vain to know them. Sometimes, I resigned myself to watching them as they came and went, but I was beginning to feel uterly helpless in these strange surroundings.

Hitherto I had always managed to feel at home, no matter where I might be. I had learned to sleep at any hour of the day or night, had eaten what was put before me, and had never felt discouraged. India had taught me patience during my two years at Calcutta, for I had discovered that the Hindi word, *kal,* may mean "yesterday" as well as "tomorrow" the difference being expressed in the written phrase by the tense of the verb, and in conversation by a movement of the head or an inflexion of the voice. It had taken me weeks to learn how to use this subtle rule correctly.

For another example, no one in India will ever say "No", which might mean losing face; or "Yes", which might well be presumptuous, since one cannot see into the future. I had questioned dozens of people on this point, from learned swamis to illiterate peasant women, and had always been brought back to the same practical philosophy. Time, they said, is ours only for the duration of a breath. The present is very short, yet regarded in the abstract it is as vast as space. *'Kala* (time),' the peasant said, 'is something which I can neither see nor grasp, but Kâlî, the terrible, great Goddess, I know well, for in Her hands are all the attributes of life, and Her heart knows all our longings and our fears. Only Kâlî can deliver me from the chain to which I am bound.' Moreover, Panditji himself had said, 'Change the level of your consciousness, and you will find that time is no more than the seat of experience, which is the ultimate reality of life.' That is how I, too, had learned to say *"Atcha!"* like all the rest. *"Atcha!"* that magical word, affirming nothing and denying nothing, simply stating, "I am here!"

As I meditated on Panditji's suggestion that I should "change the level of my consciousness", I wondered what I could possibly do to bring about such a result, for I could not find words to express my feelings at receiving that piece of advice. All that I could manage was to repeat over and over again the questions which most Hindus ask themselves, "What have I achieved in my life?" "How have I failed?" and "What next?"

I had seen Hindus go off on long pilgrimages in the hopes of discovering those all-important answers, and others, who had spent several days sitting at the feet of a guru, had returned looking serenely at peace with their inmost selves, and had then taken up their lives again in middle-class India, where conditions are far more difficult than in Europe. In large Indian towns salaries are low, housing wretched, food dear and of bad quality. The unemployed wander about the streets and the noise is unceasing. In such overpopulated cities, people sleep on the pavements in the whirling smoke of charcoal braziers, and women wash their clothes under the fire-hydrants. Men must live, no matter how, no matter what the cost. There are too many people everywhere.

The question "What have I achieved?" was the one for me. It obtruded itself more and more urgently as I considered the years which I had spent in studying the Sacred Texts, my repeated journeys to India, and my visits to those exclusive communities, which they call ashrams, where the disciples of a Holy Man devote themselves to a Master's ideal, as he teaches them to progress along the way of true understanding. Like some Bengalis who live in the delta of the Ganges, I felt a longing to trace the entire course of the river to its source, and there bathe, so that I might live the experience with all my being. Each year thousands of pilgrims take the road, without fear of attack by robbers or extremes of heat and cold. They are moved by one idea, to retain strength, which flows out of them as the river flows down to the sea, until they reach the high valleys of the Gahwhal, where the Ganges has its source. The pilgrimage entails a gradual relinquishment of personality, until at last nothing is left but the heart of the True Self, and every step becomes a victory. The meaning had become clear to me since my arrival at Shanti Bhavan.

The fact that I was foreign to everything had forced me to shed all my old habits, for ordinary gestures, impulses and good manners were wrong in these surroundings. But I could hardly remain passive. Still less could I insist on their accepting my normal ways. Moreover, I felt when I talked with the men of the family that they had some motivating force, which might become mine if only I could find the means to capture it, but which might very easily elude me. If that happened, how calamitous for me, who had travelled so far to learn what I could not understand, but could clearly sense in the people around me.

I tried to satisfy myself with such scraps of teaching as I could assimilate, but could never obtain the fuller information for which my Western mind was craving. Everything then became muddled, and I felt more than usually clumsy, stupid, and insecure. Whenever we met, the Uncle-of-the-Gîtâ said the same thing. 'You simply must stop your thinking-machine, then you will understand your emotions better. Emotions arise out of forces which you should learn to recognize, for then, you will do nothing unnecessary either outwardly or inwardly. You will be mistress of yourself and at peace. Your impulses will look after themselves when you cease to let your mind interfere with them. Try, and you will see.'

'What will happen then?'

He laughed and, as always, answered with a smile. 'You will be as tranquil as a mountain pool, instead of being thrown by the tide on every shore, the slave of every passing influence. You will also be much closer to your True Self. It will be a start, at any rate.'

Had I read these words in a book, they would probably have meant nothing to me, but something new was happening, for both Panditji and the uncle had been talking as though I were a member of the family, urging me to be ever watchful to recapture the natural self that had been mind before it was remoulded by habit and social conventions.

That was what had caused my distress. It was the effort to make friends with this Self of which I knew nothing, except that it took every possible opportunity to disappear. At that time, I had not been able to understand that the answer lay in the conflict when the Self separates from the personality.

One evening, Panditji's wife, Sakuntala as I had at last discovered, said to me: 'From the way you walk, anyone would think that your heels were dead. They must hurt the ground.'

'How ought they to be?'

'They should be as soft and supple as the palm of your hand, and come down differently upon earth or sand or mud. Can you tell the difference when you tread upon a grain of rice or a piece of gravel?'

I looked at my heels, which had been hardened by walking barefoot in my room, or in loose sandals outside. Until then, I had never given the matter a thought.

'They keep us in touch with mother earth,' said Sakuntala. 'It is like being far from home when we do not feel this contact with her.'

She hesitated for words. 'When you first enter your new family as a young bride,' she continued, 'you feel half-dead with fright as the older ones gather round you. Some kind sister-in-law says, "See! she walks like an elephant," for the elephant is a dignified animal and has a beautifully balanced walk. Then someone else adds, "She jumps about like a frog or a monkey, or wriggles like a snake." Each animal has its characteristic motion, just as life in us flows from our limbs to our hearts and heads.'

'What did this family say to you?'

'The widows said, "Put a pitcher on your head and let us see whether you sow flowers behind you like Radha,[1] or whether you dig deep ruts." You may not answer back, for new-comers have to be silent. It is a very difficult time, and everyone makes fun of you.'

She ended by saying, 'When you walk, try to remember to be light on your feet, and draw yourself in round your backbone, so that you are straight and supple like a rising flame. Otherwise, you will be caught up in all the mistakes that happen at groundlevel. They are like the creepers that cling round one's ankles in the jungle.'

As she was speaking, she began to massage my poor shapeless heels, and then my legs and back. Her fingers ran over me so lightly that I could scarcely feel them, but I understood that she was trying to teach me to be consciously alive in every part of my body, for, as she explained, 'It is only when one's heart is open that God can take up his dwelling there. Hearts are like heels, they can become as hard as stone if we do not take care of them. I wish mine were lined with mirrors, a temple filled with *prema* (the most intense love of God).'

[1] The best-loved disciple of the god Krishna.

Dear Sakuntala! with her muddled English and her similes! She had been trying to explain such useful things to me, and went away that evening all smiles, without the slighest idea that her crumbs of information only served to increase my confusion. If she is right, I thought, if every gesture is significant and reveals a state of being, I must seem to them as thick-skinned as a hippopotamus. I am so entirely ignorant.

I vented my irritation freely upon Kumar, Anil's tutor, who came very officiously every morning to inquire what I needed. The poor fellow had become my whipping-boy. Physically, he was the type of Brahmin whom I most disliked, and whom one sees so often in India, a sly nervous, slip of a man. He thought that I had no business at Shanti Bhavan and showed his feelings in little ways, for example, by coming into my room as though it belonged to him. He was Panditji's *chela* or disciple, and in his sourly ingratiating manner, would have obeyed any orders that his master cared to give him. The command to attend on me made him humble and peevish. He was appallingly poor, trying to continue his education and, I am certain, supporting some old mother or aunt, or a widowed sister with children to bring up. I was old enough to be his mother.

I owe a great deal to poor Kumar, who many times acted as my watchdog, for instance, on the night when Panditji took me to a service in one of the most strictly orthodox of the temples to Vishnu, where he announced his arrival with "members of his household". Foreigners were strictly forbidden inside, but nevertheless, so far as Kumar was concerned, Panditji had every right to take me, because that was his decision. At the same time, he had to be prevented from losing face before the priests. Luckily for me, it was only after our return that I discovered the ban on foreigners, for Kumar had simply said that I came from Kashmir. I felt very awkward about having gate-crashed, and said, 'Were you not afraid that I should make a mistake? I might very easily have done so.'

Indeed, when we had gone up to the priest after the service to have holy water poured on our hands, one false move would have betrayed me. 'No,' said Kumar coldly. 'You had only to follow the others. Woman's duty is to obey the rule exactly and you were in the right mood. Why are you worrying now over what might have happened? You are emphasizing differences, instead of remembering that we are all under one roof. There is only one thing to understand, our respective places in relation to Panditji!'

All of which amounted to saying that Panditji watched the danger signals for us, and that we were simply his instruments. He overheard this conversation, but his face was quite expressionless. I said no more, because I knew how much he hated women to speak before strangers, and there was quite a large group of us going through the forest between the hill and the town. Our storm-lanterns drove the shadows before us, and in the distance, other parties could be seen making their way towards the neighbouring villages.

I could understand Panditji's rank as head of the family, but to me he remained essentially the seeker, the one who said, 'Didi, where is he who will take my hand and lead me to the end of my journey? The way is so long and I have little time!'

'But you are not yet fifty!"

'I suppose I am in a hurry.'

Ever since Panditji had discovered from the police registers that I was older than he, he had begun to call me "Didi", the pet-name for all older sisters in India. I had been annoyed at his finding out my age, because I had thought that our friendship might suffer, but on the contrary, from that day onwards, he came much more often to my room and spoke with a humility which I found very moving. Once he had said, 'The worst of all would be not to know why one was born.'

His problem seemed strangely like my own and I therefore

watched his reactions carefully, hoping to set my course by his. I realized that the rigid hierarchy of a Brahmin family, governing the status and actions of every member (even including me), was another aspect of the continuous flow of religious life, which each one interpreted according to his lights.

'The river of consciousness will never cease to flow,' Panditji had said one day, 'although man's will to imbibe it may weaken or even cease for a time. Republican India, so eager to change the old ways in order to achieve a higher standard of living, may possibly turn away from ancient traditions and become completely materialistic. Though that state of affairs may last for several centuries, nothing can change the unchanging. India had already known long periods of religious denial, when every belief has been questioned. Perhaps India itself may disappear, together with its towns and temples, and even all our families. Anything is possible as the waves rise and fall. Yet the great Law, that reigns supreme over destruction and creation, will continue to be, even although the human spirit cannot conceive its vastness and wisdom. Man can only destroy the life which he transmits, whereas God creates life and gives it unceasingly on every plane. That is a work of pure Love—true and inconceivable. Our life abounds with such miracles.'

On another occasion, Panditji had said, 'The vast store of pure wisdom which India keeps hidden will survive all destruction, for some will always choose to devote themselves wholly to fulfilling the Law, without concern for the actuality that binds our lives to the present. A chosen few, especially from our caste (because our traditions incline us in that direction), have always been preserved for this calling. They live in caves or ashrams, alone, or in the world, and their sacrifice is made with full awareness so that others, much later perhaps, may in their turn gain knowledge.' Thus Panditji, himself something of a seer, led me deep into his inmost thoughts.

In everyday life, he was amused by my prickly relationship

with Kumar, and he knew about our squabbles because we each complained of the other. Yet he did nothing to make things easier for us. 'Kumar is an ass,' he used to say, 'He is obstinate and self-opinionated, in fact, he has every fault I lack, and when I am with him I feel complete. I know that he does not like you, but that is his own affair. He will serve you unquestioningly because you are one of us. Why not get him to teach you Hindi grammar? It will be a fine opportunity for you, because he needs two hundred rupees to pay the farmers in his village and will therefore be here until the autumn.'

Panditji also said, 'I shall take you, with Anil and Kumar, to some of the mountain temples that contain living exponents of the divine wisdom. Anil has not yet seen them. It will be a chance for both of you. We shall start tomorrow.'

I knew, however, that when he said "tomorrow", he meant, "Later, when you understand; when you are ready to appreciate." That, at any rate, was what I took his meaning to be, for nothing happened. He might even have meant, "When the rains come," or, just as likely, "When Anil passes his examination." One thing that I did know for sure was that I should be told of his decision five minutes before leaving, because only one person's wishes counted, his own.

I had already learned that one should at all times be prepared to obey an order from above, but not out of slavish obedience or respect for tradition, as might well have been supposed. On such occasions something quite different emerged. Force was suddenly generated, the perfect moment arrived to unite with a higher Law and take flight towards new knowledge.

Ashok, who did not readily share his thoughts with me, sometimes gave me explanations as we went for our walks. 'Each thought,' he said, 'each impulse, arises in a *nâdî*[1] of our

[1] A *nâdî* is a nerve that is subtly different from those belonging to the nervous system.

bodies. Each *nâdî* controls an inward feeling that has its own particular vibration. You will learn to recognize a fresh harmony, a thrill which you have not yet felt. When that happens, you cannot go wrong; for it is the voice of truth.

'What about you?' I asked, 'Do you have this sensation?' but Ashok evaded my question, merely repeating with much earnestness, 'You must be prepared at all times; that is all-important.'

I felt suddenly afraid, but of what I could not have said, for my mind was in confusion. Ashok had also said, 'Every impulse that comes from below must be recognized and rejected, no matter how insignificant. You cannot cheat yourself. That is not a question of morality, but of common sense and self-respect. Why should you try to deceive yourself?'

'Does everyone here follow that rule?'

'Everyone knows it, but each one reacts according to his own evolution. We are all reminded several times a day by what you call our "Brahmin taboos",' he added, laughing. 'You think of them as interfering with the liberty of the individual, whereas to us, they are measuring-rods by which disciplined men test themselves in ordinary everyday life. Mahommedans have their prayers, which record the passing hours five times a day.'

I, too, felt those continual reminders of the Law, of which Ashok had been speaking. Every time that I ate alone in my room I remembered them, because they cut me off from what I had been doing only a moment before, with Panditji or the uncle, and abruptly returned to my own sphere, which I might otherwise have forgotten. There were other rules that gave to each day its own especial flavour. Once a fortnight, for example, there was the day when one took sacrifices to the temple, another when one did not leave home, days for visiting friends, and others for fasting. The days themselves contained certain hours, fixed by the religious calendar, which were devoted to work or meditation, etc. Had it merely been a question of rules, I should have revolted. But these were laws, and regulated life as integral parts of a far greater, more all-embracing Law. Under their governance I might, perhaps, find my own "moment of opportunity".

To Naraïn, I was still a source of perpetual anxiety. He thought me an irresponsible female, who went out to the bazaar to buy fountain-pen ink whenever she pleased. He very soon, however, discovered a way of controlling my movements, and his method was simplicity itself—he hid my sandals and returned them two hours later, with a patient smile and a bowl of scalding tea. When I scolded him, he would merely repeat, over and over again, 'Bhagavan, Bhagavan . . .' which means, "Oh! Lord!, Oh! Lord! . . ."

After a time he began to realize that I was not trying to play truant, and that the entire family knew when I went out to buy toothpaste, paper, or a new ribbon for my typewriter.

8

Lakshmi, the Madwoman

It was Ashok who first took me to visit Uncle Biren, Maharaj's son and from that day onwards, my position in the family completely changed.

He was about fifty years old, and lived in the south wing of Ananda Bhavan in a room almost entirely lined with documents tied up with red tape. It looked like any one of the thousands of passport offices that you find in India, overflowing with official records, all neatly filed and labelled. Uncle Biren was a retired lawyer, but still concerned with certain law-suits and the administration of a public transport company; he also sat as honorary chairman on the boards of various schools and orphanages. He was a warm-hearted man, rather dictatorial, and always in a tremendous hurry.

He quickly told me that his two married daughters had graduated in law and economics, and that his sons were still at the universities of Delhi and Allahabad. Uncle Biren prided himself upon the modernity of his outlook, and preached the emancipation of young people. It was entirely owing to him that the women of the family were allowed to go out without a servant in attendance and to do their own shopping in the bazaar. On the question of marriage, however, he remained inflexible. That, he considered, was a matter for the parents. The wedding which Maharaj had mentioned was that of his youngest daughter.

Uncle Biren wished to know where I had lived during the war. 'At a little farm in the South of France,' I answered, 'working like a peasant on the land. You see, we had to go to the earth for everything we ate.'

'So you have already come into contact with our Mother, the Earth.'

I was pleased with his answer, glad to find that he associated me with the part that woman plays in the essential nature of prakriti, primordial matter. To Hindus, this represents the Mother Divine in all her various manifestations, and woman is symbolical of nature, on the plane of human existence.

Panditji joined us as we were drinking tea. He wanted to show me the *gotra* that traced the family back to a legendary sage of earliest times, whose name was repeated each morning in the family prayers. After they had won their lands by conquest and fought fiercely with other Brahmin families, who had come to the highlands at about the same period, the opposing sides joined together to form an extremely close society.

When the *gotra* was spread out on the ground, it looked like an oriental carpet. It represented a tree with strange birds perched on the branches and fish and serpents gliding among the roots. Each leaf was covered with minute *devanagari*[1] writing, recording the history of a lifetime. Little Ganthu already had a leaf for himself, but it was still as white as a new passport. Most of the leaves were painted blue or green, but one or two yellow ones were scattered here and there among them. In one corner there was an explanatory key; blue leaves indicated members of the family who, in different generations, had taken vows of complete renunciation, either as swâmis or sannyasins. Some of them had left home at a very early age in search of a guru, a spiritual director capable of leading them towards the fulfilment of the "Great Aim".

Those who had been priests or administrators of temple-

---

[1] *Devanagari*, the characters in which Sanskrit is usually written.

property, and all their descendants, had green leaves, and so had lawyers and civil servants. Yellow ones stood for those who had "lost their senses, or the way", in other words, who had done something discreditable, or had voluntarily served the English! Startled, I looked up at Panditji, but he had put on his obstinate expression, to avoid questions. He carefully rolled up the *gotra,* touched his forehead with it as a sign of respect, and shut it away in a small iron box, along with other family treasures.

While we were talking, other men had entered the room quite silently, for they were barefooted, and had sat down in groups upon the floor, after one of the servants had brought them each a small, square rug. The design of these was clearly of Tibetan or Chinese origin, like Uncle Biren's writing-table, a high wooden desk, with carvings and highly-coloured paintings on a pale blue ground.

The men had evidently come to discuss the news. Some of them smoked a Hookah, which they passed from hand to hand. The main subject of conversation was the problem of admitting a large company of refugee-Sikhs to the district, and the privileges which it would be proper to allow them. There was a good deal of opposition from the bazaar shopkeepers, who had booths along the whole of the ancient paved road that ran from one end of the town to the other. They also discussed the new road for motor-coaches, which was to extend deep into the surrounding country, where they were sure that the Sikhs would quickly set up restaurants and tea-rooms. Hitherto the town had possessed only one restaurant, for the custom of eating out had not yet reached high-caste families.

We were all sitting, I being the only woman present, when suddenly a Hindu girl wearing a red sarî came resolutely in, with a garland of flowers. Not looking in the least shy, she went straight to Uncle Biren, greeting him with affectionate respect, making it obvious that she was his daughter. Next she came to me and after a ceremonial bow, put the garland round my neck. It was a chain of roses and gardenias, each petal of which had been turned back. I at once felt something strange in the atmosphere and cast a glance at Panditji, but, as always, when things became difficult, he vanished, leaving me to surmount the obstacles as best I could. The girl smiled, she had a beautiful face, quite smooth and unlined. Then, in excellent English, she said coaxingly, 'Have you seen my Nath? Can you give me news of him? Can you tell me when he is coming home? I have not heard from him for so long.'

Then I understood. I took her hand and said, 'What is your name?'

'Lakshmi!'

'What a pretty name! It is that of the Goddess of Plenty, is it not? I am sure you know how to draw her *alpona*. Will you show me?' I was speaking of the symbolical design that women trace each morning by the house-door with grains of rice, as a courtesy to the first visitor. Then I led her out of the circle of busy men to the far end of the room, where we could talk quietly.

'When Nath comes home', said Lakshmi, 'I shall not draw an *alpona* for him. Nath is not a guest, he is my husband, and I wait all day and all night to greet him with flowers. He said he would come back. Everybody I meet I ask for news of him, but nobody has seen him.'

Two boys of between fifteen and twenty years old had followed us. One said, 'My sister is a little mad. Her husband died after they had been married for a few weeks, and she lost her reason. Now she is home again, but she lives all the time in a dream.'

'I want to show you my sarîs,' said Lakshmi, 'I have some beauties and I will give you one.' At this, the youngest brother made a dash for the dark passage by which we had entered, and I wondered whether he had gone for assistance, or to obtain permission, but he soon returned, saying 'My eldest sister would be glad to see you.'

He ushered me out into the passage and pulled back a curtain on the left-hand side. I found myself on a sunny terrace, where five women were winnowing rice with bamboo fans. Several children played around them. They made a rush for me to exchange courtesies, there were introductions all round and a good deal of nervous giggling. One of the women said with an air of authority, 'As soon as Lakshmi saw you coming, she began to make a garland. Now she has gone to fetch some tea. Come and see my room while we are waiting,' and she led me into another room.

This girl looked about thirty years old, and I could see by the heavy bunch of keys that hung from the edge of her sarî that she was mistress of the house, a fact for which she apologized, because I was the elder. 'We have been longing to meet you,' she said, 'but I ought to warn you that I have had no university training, because there has never been time. My husband gives me tuition every evening so that I may pass my school finals, after which I can continue my education. That is absolutely necessary, is it not? I have read Ruskin, and am beginning *Les Misérables*. That is because of you, I want to know about your country.'

'Tell me about your keys,' I said. 'They look to me like signs of a much better training than any number of university courses.'

'Oh!' she answered, 'I am responsible for Ananda Bhavan. My two brothers-in-law are still students and unmarried, in any case, they belong to the new generation. They will marry later, when they have their degrees, and their wives will also have university diplomas. That is essential now-a-days. My little sisters and cousins all go to college. Aruna, who is going to be married in ten days' time, has already passed her law-examinations.'

As she spoke, she made me sit down cross-legged upon the bed, facing her. We leaned our elbows on fat bolsters covered with *broderie Anglaise*. Lakshmi brought us tea and went quickly away. My heart-to-heart talk with the young mistress of Ananda Bhavan was of immense value, because it was an initiation into the life of the women. I ate little fried cakes slowly, without speaking. Protima, as my hostess was called, gazed at me and said nothing. Her frank, smiling face seemed to encourage questions, for, as the elder, it was my turn to speak first.

'Have you been married long?'

'For fifteen years. My mother-in-law died suddenly a few months later, but the widows who live here helped me to learn my duties because I was only just sixteen at that time. I could not speak any English then, for my father was very strictly orthodox and would not let me go to school or learn foreign languages. It was my husband who encouraged me to work, and I go on with my studies. Here are my books; I have several others as well,' she added, pointing to a shelf full of grammars and text-books.

I soon realized that what most interested Protima was the number of books which she had read, the number of examinations passed, and the variety of subjects she had studied. She spoke a mid-Victorian kind of English at breakneck speed, and did not listen to anything that I said. She had fallen victim to the passion for diplomas, so prevalent among Hindu women, for she was one of those who formed a bridge between two generations. With her keys and her elementary education she stood between her mother and grandmother, who had had a traditional upbringing without contact with the outside world, and her ten-year-old grand-daughter who in due course would go to the university.

All the business of the house passed through Protima's hands. She looked after Uncle Biren, Maharaj, the ten other people living in the house, and all the servants, both indoor and outdoor. The food, the seeds for the farmers, the organization of numerous festivals, when more than a hundred guests were catered for, all came within the scope of her duties. Most of the family weddings were celebrated at Ananda Bhavan, because it contained a "marriage-chamber", with a gallery from which spectators might look on at entertainments in the court-yard below, as though they were in some large theatre. All these were the concern of Protima, and she had three children to bring up as well.

Lakshmi's mental condition had relieved her of all family-duties and obedience to the hierarchy. She came and went among the men as the children did, living as she pleased, strew-ing about her the small tokens of her love. 'In love, there is no one like her,' said Protima. And it was true, for the devotion of Lakshmi was such, that her darling Nath, for whom she searched endlessly, even going down to the town to question travellers, sometimes came alive in her heart. There, he sat upon a golden throne shaped like a lotus and filled her with the joy of his presence. At such times, she lived in an ecstasy which lasted for several days. She ceased to be tormented, and sang sublimely for her Nath, accompanying herself on a zither, with words that brought tears to the eyes of those who heard her.

The singing-master, a blind actor who also taught elocu-tion, said that she had a genius for upsetting all the traditional rhythms but never made a mistake in her chosen mode. Sure instinct guided her. 'Ah!' he used to say, 'if only Lakshmi could know what she feels, she would be a very great artist. One day, perhaps, her mind will tell her why she grieves, then she will be able to control her singing, the child of her suffer-ing will be born, and she will be saved.'

Lakshmi had arranged a little temple where she worshipped the Lord Krishna, in whose care she had placed Nath, when he went to London to take his finals. He had been killed in a motorbus accident. When they broke the news she had merely smiled, saying, 'Nath told me that he would soon be home. I have more faith than you. I know that he will come back.' She had refused to give up her jewels and silken sarîs or to fast

like other widows, and, soon afterwards, she had begun to sing
for Nath; something which she had never done before he left
her.

Protima talked freely of all these happenings. The room in
which we sat was her private kingdom. Advertisement-calen-
dars with pictures of the gods hung on the walls, books and
exercise-books overflowed from the bookshelves, clothes and
sarîs were draped over the bed. There was nothing of beauty,
nothing even pleasant to look at, but Protima did the honours
like a reigning queen.

I began to wonder whether I ought to cut short my visit, or
whether it was for her to end it. I was still trying to decide,
when several women burst into the room followed by Lakshmi
with her sarîs. They were laughing and elbowing one another
and all chattering at once. In a moment they had surrounded
me, and were undressing me and taking down my hair. They
decided to plait it with ribbons and to teach me to wear my
sarî in the local fashion. When each had added something to
the new arrangement of my hair, had oiled it, blackened my
eyelids, placed a red spot upon my forehead, painted the soles
of my feet with carmine and the backs of my hands with pads
dipped in a paste of sandalwood, they sat me upon the bed in
a traditional pose, with garlands round my neck and arms.
Then they ran laughing to fetch Panditji and Uncle Biren, and
when everyone had arrived, they all began to talk loudly and
excitedly in Hindi. They were obviously delighted with their
efforts.

Panditji told them about my typewriter, my note-books, and
the card-index that lay on my table. 'Yes!' he said, 'she has
even made a lampshade with her cards.' There was a great deal
of talk about lampshades in Kurmachala, where electricity
had just arrived. They were being sold in the bazaar at quite
exorbitant prices. Most of the wiring was very rudimentary,
still at the stage of naked bulbs dangling at the end of a flex.
This piece of modern equipment in Protima's room with its

carved panelling, and windows with fretted columns in the Nepalese style, struck me as ugly and incongrous.

'I will show you how to make them if you like.'

'When? Now?'

So I spent the whole of that day at Ananda Bhavan, cutting lampshades out of stiff paper, which had been sent for from the town, together with glue and paper-clips.

Night had fallen before I returned to my room, escorted by two servants carrying lanterns. Lakshmi had given me one of her sarîs, pale blue-grey silk to match my eyes and Krishna's heaven, where Nath, her beloved Nath, was staying, as she thought, a little too long.

9

I Cross The Threshold

İT WAS ON THE FOLLOWING DAY THAT I FIRST CROSSED THE inner threshold. I had gone down to Panditji's room to study a text which we were proposing to translate from the Hindi (he into English and I into French), when Mataji entered with her heavy tread, as characteristic as her thick, rather slow speech. She was wearing gold-rimmed glasses. She gave me a great slap on the back with the flat of her hand, a gesture of affection which Panditji interpreted thus. 'My mother has come to fetch you. Go and put on a silk sarî, she will wait.'

I rose and left the room, to return soon afterwards more suitably dressed. Mataji made a sign for me to follow.

Panditji's study led into Mataji's room, which, in turn, opened on to the inner courtyard. The room was large and rather dark, furnished only by two beds placed side by side to form a highly polished platform on which people might sit. The pillows, rolled in coverlets, served as bolsters on which to prop the elbows. Two or three low bookcases, glassed and padlocked, were fixed to the wall near some sequin-covered pictures of the gods.

Mataji led me towards a doorway leading into a small and ancient glass veranda, with several panes broken. Near the door stood gardening tools and a box of seedlings. 'Mind the step,' said Mataji, pushing me in front of her. Suddenly, I found myself standing before the family gods, and was so little expecting them that I felt utterly taken aback. I had wrongly supposed that the family would have had a chapel, equipped in a style to match the luxury and good taste among which they lived. This was not so, however, for their private religion was an inward kind of worship, accompanied by only a few ritual practices. These took place between the bedroom and the charcoal fires that smoked in the outside courtyard, in that little alcove, among sacks of rice, pots of melted butter hanging in nets from the ceiling, and clothes lying in the sun to dry.

There was a straw mat, on which I sat beside Mataji as we bowed before the gods and touched the floor with our foreheads. I saw before me the conch-shell, the copper pot for ablutions, and the sticks of incense. A little farther off, in the centre of the floor, was a three-legged stool with a tray for the morning offering of flower petals, blades of grass, leaves of basil, pieces of coconut, sugar-cane, and chopped fruit. In the middle, a pierced bronze casket stood open, in which I could see several tiny copper figurines, images of the household gods. Each member of the family, I thought, must have his own, his special means of approach to the Supreme Being. That God of gods, on this humble altar was symbolized by a salagrama, one of those black, oval stones, found by some of the rivers of Nepal. This particular pebble, which had been given the place of honour, was smaller than an egg. Its function was to aid meditation at each level of consciousness, for thought strays amid forms of ever-increasing purity, until finally it reaches pure abstraction. The stone evoked no images, its sole purpose was to concentrate the effort towards perception. How far I had travelled from the wildly exuberant shapes and forms in the sculptures and bas-reliefs of the great temples and porticoes of Southern India, the processions of kings, nymphs, beasts and gigantic gods! Such images are gradually abandoned as nature becomes more stark, until one reaches the great snow-mountains, where stone reigns supreme, worn smooth and polished by the action of wind and water.

Mataji invited me to repeat after her the following Sanskrit words, which she pronounced very slowly, so that I might understand them:

> *'Glory to Purusha, the Spirit that is beyond form,*
> *The Inconceivable, the Immanent.*
> *I invoke thee in the name of Vishnu,*
> *Who is closer to me,*
> *And whose attributes I know.*
> *Pardon my desire for knowledge,*
> *My longing to approach thee,*
> *For I come in all humility.*
> *Suffering and poverty vanish before thee,*
> *All is stillness and purity.*
> *Oh! Lord of Light,*
> *Day and night, I commit errors innumerable,*
> *Forgive me, thy servant,*
> *For I have no other refuge than in thee.*
> *Oh! Lord! be merciful to me!*
> *I bring thee flower-offerings and hymns of praise.*
> *May the five gods, of whom Vishnu is the chief,*
> *Be appeased!*
> *My lips utter their names . . .'*

As she continued the prayer alone, Mataji took the sala-grama, raised it to her forehead, touched mine, and put it into my cupped hands. Then, replacing it upon the tray she said, 'You are a woman, my sister, born far from here upon a distant shore. May the Living Spirit enter you. May it penetrate your mind and heart, your very womb. May it dwell within you. Then you shall know something really true.'

Mataji was quick and neat. She took the tray in both hands,

and saying another prayer, marked my forehead with sandal-wood. Then she touched my eyes, nostrils, ears, and lips with water. She put into my mouth crumbs of all the different foods that had been offered to the gods that morning. She placed a flower upon my head, and others in my hands and in front of me. I felt deeply moved as I watched her, for she was investing me with new dignity. When she had finished, she put down the tray and bowed low before me.

I did nothing to prevent her for, indeed, I was as fixed as any image. This lasted an appreciable time, and then, without more ado, we came on to terms of extreme intimacy. Mataji proceeded, none too gently, to correct my posture. She straightened my back, slid her fingers between each of my ribs to discover how I was breathing, and rapped my neck, which was too stiff and tense for her liking. She altered the position of my hands, spread my fingers apart, and finished by teaching me to say the morning prayer, counting out the syllables upon my knuckles. It was extraordinarily difficult, because one had to pay attention to so many things at once, breathing, intonation, pronunciation, rhythm, and all the while sit perfectly still and relaxed. Each muscle had to be flexible, so that another "presence" might enter.

When I rose, it was my turn to bow to Mataji. I hardly knew how to express my gratitude, for now she had become my own "Mataji". We went out into the court, where Naraïn lay in the sun with his back propped against a pillar. Sakuntala and another woman were washing clothes. She made a friendly gesture, wagging her head at me and I answered in the same way, but I was in a hurry to return to my own room, for I was overflowing with all that had happened and longing to be alone. I was tired and sleepy. Also, I was hungry.

10

Women

FROM THAT DAY ONWARDS I WORKED WITH THE WOMEN OF the house when they sorted the corn and rice. I went with them taking offerings to the temple, received callers, and visited the other women of the family. I attended the classes when pandits came to give them lessons in music, verse-making, Sanskrit, or religious drama. I was also allowed to play with the children.

With each pursuit I crossed a new threshold of traditional Hindu family life, and learned the importance of each gesture in its complicated mechanism. No detail is left to chance, even the most ordinary everyday actions are included in religious duties.

The rice arrived in bales, straight from the villages. It was then thrashed out by the servants and poured into great shallow copper troughs, from which we took it by the sieve-full when we sorted it. Part of it, whole grains of equal size, was put aside for distinguished guests or temple priests, when there were festivals in honour of the Divine Mother.

I loved those hours spent in rice-sorting, when we sat in a circle on straw mats in the inner court. I liked feeling my whole body relax, and the sound of tinkling bracelets as the sieves were swung from right to left with measured rhythmical movements. I enjoyed listening to the chatter, hearing the high voices of the younger women against the heavier tones of older generations, watching the lovely sheen on the materials, and the contrast between the light skins of the women and their sarîs, which were often of some dark colour, green, or the blue of distant woods.

They talked very loud and very fast; it was a puzzle to know how they managed to understand each other in that babble. In the midst of their rapid, continuous movements, came sudden interruptions as one bowed deeply to another, meaning "Forgive me if I knocked you!" When a newcomer arrived, voices were hushed, as she made the sweeping, open-handed gesture, bowing very low to touch the feet of her elders. This very formal piece of politeness taught me that, on account of age, I came seventh in rank, between the widows and the young women, and that I, too, must make the deep gesture of respect to those older than myself.

On certain days, a two-handled iron cauldron half-full of sand was heated on a tripod. The rice was thrown into it and stirred quickly about with a long-handled iron spoon. It leaped and popped and swelled, and became crisp and golden. I thought it very good when we ate it at the evening meal with "gour", the rough, sticky, brown sugar that filled so many baskets in the bazaar.

No one now treated me as a stranger. The talk revolved chiefly around two subjects, journeys to the plains and pilgrimages. Kurmachala was the collecting point for caravans bound northwards for the foot of Mount Kailas, in Tibet, and for those going to Kedarnath and Badrinath, in the opposite direction. Most of the women had sons, whose local education was finished and who were about to spend several years at the Universities of Allahabad and Lucknow. They would henceforward be at home only during vacations.

One day as we were working, we were visited by a young Tibetan princess, aged about eighteen, who had left her home, a palace of mud and stone, for the first time. She and her suite had come down from the high plateau of the Himalayas, with

a caravan of mules laden with borax, and was on her way to
Delhi to take the aeroplane for London. She had seen neither
cars, motor-coaches, nor trains, and appeared quite incurious
about them all. Educated, as she had been, to seek for the
absolute that embraces all things, she took in her stride the
various surprises which life brought her. She thought it perfectly natural, for instance, to go the quickest way to pursue
her study of mathematics, and sailed into the midst of modern
engineering with an open mind and no preconceived ideas to
hinder her acceptance of new inventions. As one of the family
said, 'After all, King Râma flew in his *pushpaka*.[1] There is
nothing new, it has all been written in the Vedas.'

Indeed these people were surprised by nothing, for everything was part of the perpetual movement of life, in which
nothing is permanent. The women of the family shared experiences that were happening far away, and lived them not
only in imagination but also in their hearts. The lives of Mrs.
Pandit and Princess Amrit Kaur (an ambassadress and a min-
ister of the Indian government) belonged to them as much
as did the lives of their own children. These two outstanding
women are supported by the thoughts of millions of high-caste
women who, themselves, are encouraged by the hopes and
longings of countless others less highly educated. Such is the
Law. My Western ideas often prevented me from realizing how
strongly the women of India feel conscious of their interde-
pendence, even although I had a limited but perfect example
before me in the family life at Shanti Bhavan. I still, however,
instinctively recoiled at the attitude of Hindu women, and
could feel at one with them only when their babies, no longer
frightened by my white skin, climbed on my lap and put their
arms round my neck.

Only a few of my own generation could speak English.

[1] *Pushpaka:* a flying machine, described in the Râmâyana, and
supposed to have been a forerunner of the aeroplane.

Most of them had married very young and were already grand-mothers, some even were widows. When I first arrived, they had all been very reserved towards me until the day when Uncle Biren had said that they might take me to the temple.

After that, there had come a torrent of friendly criticism and kindness, until I, myself, was forced to draw back, for they appeared to lose all sense of tact or proportion. They began coming into my room at all hours of the day, bringing books and photographs. They read my letters and settled down with their knitting beside my table to watch me as I worked. Every word and action of mine was reported back to the rest of the family. If they liked my sarîs, they took them and tried them on; yet I was helpless to prevent them, because they were so completely unself-conscious. There was nothing that I could do.

One evening, however, when they had completely ex-hausted me, I told my troubles to Ashok, to his utter astonish-ment. 'But what do you mean by your own property?' he said at length. 'A letter is an impression that comes to you from outside, like the food you eat, or the air you breathe. None of these things belongs to you personally. In different degrees, they are necessary to your physical life. You could not do without them, but they are not part of your real self. Can you find nothing to unite you to our lives? When my cousins bound that yellow silk thread round your wrist, they joined your life to theirs. That bond is as strong as any blood relation-ship. Cannot you be your real self and break down this barrier of personal privacy?'

I could find no answer. 'Have they hurt your sense of possession?' continued Ashok, 'your love of order and of the *status quo?* What I should call your Western love of power, which has hitherto been so strong an influence in your life?'

I knew to what Ashok was referring. A few days earlier, he had taken me with Kumar to a country village where he had business with one of the five members of the *Panchayat,* the local administrative council. On our way, we had passed some peasants' houses with beautifully carved façades, in which the rotten wood had been patched with sheets of corrugated iron, with disastrous effect. There was a low, broken-down wall nearby, surrounding a sycamore tree at the foot of which some red-painted stones and a few shreds of coloured cloth, tied to twigs, indicated one of the many local shrines, ruined, battered by wind and rain, but still functioning. Some rotting coconuts and the wicks of oil-lamps lay among Shivaite iron tridents. One sweep of a good broom would have made this little natural temple tidy and reverent, and I let Ashok see my disapproval.

Nothing was said, however, and we continued on our way. 'You would like India to correspond with European ideas,' said Ashok later. 'You would prefer to see our antiquities as clean and tidy as they appear in the Victoria and Albert Museum, whereas here we live in a land of stone. Rough and undressed, it rises out of the earth, a symbol of the Divine Power. In the plains, men have built great temples, vast halls for worship with thousands of columns. They have strung sculptured shrines side by side like beads in a necklace, as though they hung together on one prayer, *"Namah Shivaya"* (I bow to Shiva). That jungle of forms and images expresses the thousand aspects of the Divine Essence. It is one of life's spiritual paradoxes that the higher you climb, the more stark and pure forms become. Here forms have no existence, except in the worship of the Holy Ones. Our Himalayan mountains are themselves the homes of the gods, indeed, it is said that they are Embodiments of the Divine, that always have and always will provide refuge for the ascetics, yogis, and holy men, who seek its shelter. The *thirtas,* the holy shrines, are full of the influence of those who have won liberation, so much so, indeed, that even atheists and agnostics are irresistibly seized by the sense of the Divine Presence concealed in this vast stretch of mountains. The stories of wild beasts that do not disturb the meditations of yogis are true, for such hermits become part and parcel of Nature herself. The fire of austerity (*tapas*) consumes forms until nothing remains of them but the desire for pure Being. Do you know what Being means? It means discovering what one really is.'

But it was more especially from the women that I hoped to learn a rule of life, and I received my first lesson on the evening when Sakuntala said, 'Didi, will you teach me how to meditate?'

'What!'

'Yes, to meditate,' repeated Sakuntala, without noticing my utter astonishment. Could she be laughing at me, I wondered, for how could a Brahmin woman ask such a question of me? I felt that there might have been some mistake of wording, and hesitated as I tried to frame an answer. Then, like a crowd of pilgrims from all parts of India coming to see the vision of the One in the Temple of the Heart, all my instincts and longings suddenly forced from me the only possible response to that unexpected question—the salutation, *Jai Kedar Nath!* (Hail! Lord of Lords!).

I thought of the great pilgrimage to Kedar Nath, which all Hindus hope to make at least once in a lifetime, and during which awareness of the eternal unity of the Supreme Essence, in all its myriad forms, comes to those mortified by fatigue. Panditji had been telling us of one old woman, who had returned from her fourteenth pilgrimage, and of a blind beggar, who had climbed the mountain beside wealthy men who refused the comfort of litters and bearers, preferring to trudge with bleeding feet, repeating the mantra of life, *"Jai Kedar Nath!"*

Like Sakuntala, I, too, was wondering how best to meditate on the "Indivisible aspect of Shiva", who is worshipped under the name of Savashiva, in his mountain-temple. Savashiva, indeed, was the patron of the entire district, and we both longed

to have his *darshan,* to come face to face with him in heart
and mind.

The aim of both of us was so to rule our lives, that we
might, even once, have contact with the Divine Being, and
that aspiration made a strong bond. That was why I was able
to answer her question by asking another. 'And now, little
sister, will you teach me to be aware of the life within me?'

'It is easy enough to try,' she said, 'the difficulty is to succeed,
for at such times a thousand crows always seem to be cawing
and tumbling around one's head.'

What she said was more than an illustration, for at that
time of the year, flights of dark birds passed overhead three or
four times a day, rending the air with harsh cries. Now that I
had learned to know Sakuntala better, she seemed to me like a
walking paradox, an example of liberty and servitude combined in one and the same person. She treated everything as
though it were holy, and by her very self-effacement had become, as the mother of four healthy sons, an active force in the
family. She was proud, and very conscious of the importance
of having secured the line of succession, and her face grew
calm and serene whenever it was mentioned.

Essentially, she was a mother, but, for Panditji, her husband, she had an almost childlike love that was very moving.
All day long, my Hindu sister thought only of serving the
Bridegroom as embodied by him. Her whole life centred
round him, and she left it to her cousins and married nieces
to keep up an appearance of independence, in the form of
demands and protests, thus showing the progressive, highly
individualistic side of some younger members of the family.
Some of the men, old as well as young, actually encouraged
the evolution of such women as felt able to fight for their independence, but the remainder silently sheltered behind tradition.

I felt the strong flow of these two opposing trends. I was in

the position of a guest, whose experience of Western civilization brought the family into touch with the outside world, but
my education had formed me in such a way that I found it
hard to imagine how my Hindu sister could combine her daily
tasks with the higher, Spiritual Life. As a matter of fact, I
never put the question to her directly. I tried to discover the
answer myself, by studying the Rule under which we both
were living, and gradually, in that part of my being where
thought and feeling merge, I found a no-man's-land, in which
arose new understanding, although I was not yet capable of
grasping it fully. Sakuntala's eyes inspired me to put the question then and, at the same time, gave me a clue to the answer.
Her way of life would give me the help which I needed.

One day, we went together to pay our respects to Srî
Govinda, a famous acharya of Benares, who was paying a
visit to a neighbouring temple. On certain days, he received
only women, in the house of one of the prominent men of the
town.

When we arrived, we went up on to the roof, where some
sheets had been spread over bamboo matting to form an awning. There were great masses of jasmine and bougainvillaea in
the court, and babies and goats upon the staircase. On all the
landings men were playing dice. They were servants, and
Naraïn, who had come as our escort, soon joined them. Saîs
were drying out of the windows and baskets of corn and other
foodstuffs cluttered the passages. As soon as we reached the
roof, however, we found an extraordinary religious peace. It
was beautiful, in the soft light cast by the awning, to see those
fifty or more women sitting upon the ground, packed closely
together, with their sarîs covering their heads. The process of
insinuating myself among them without interrupting their
devotions, of trying to unite with them in the "Song of the
Blessed" and of sharing in their intense concentration and absolute silence, aroused in me a state of consciousness which I
had at last learned to recognize. It affected my whole attitude,

the expression of my face, as well as the movements of my hands.

Srî Govinda was seated on a low wooden platform. He was teaching from the Râmâyana,[1] and like all Vaishnavas (the worshippers of Krishna) he was robed in white and wore a necklace of wooden beads on his bare breast. Beside him, a tablas-player beat out the rhythm of the verses, as he recited them in a monotonous tone. Whenever the double name of Sitâ-Râm occurred, the two long a-vowels, prolonged by the chanting of the final "m", produced a reverberation that penetrated into my very heart. Sakuntala saw that I was wincing. She gave me a nudge and whispered, 'Didi! Relax! Let the Holy Sound enter into you. Imbibe it until it actually dwells within you, until it carries you away.' I turned to look at her. She sat so still that her whole body absorbed what was happening, an attitude of such impenetrable dignity that I could see how completely she was abandoning her whole self to the primordial rumble aroused by the sound of the words. She smiled at me, took my hand, and placed it upon her right side above her breast. 'That is where "It" lives,' she whispered. 'Blessed be the Holy Name of God, and of Srî Govinda, who speaks it to us.'

When the recitation of the Holy Name was finished most of the women stole silently away, but Sakuntala, picking up her sarî, tied one corner of it round her neck and went to prostrate herself before the acharya. When she rose, she signed for me to do the same and waited. At that moment, I shared so fully in a sensation that was new to me, that for an instant I found myself expressing the Holy Name with my whole body. We returned together hand in hand.

It was I, as we separated, who said to her, 'Sakuntala, would you like us to meditate together?' She did not answer with

---

[1] The Râmâyana: The Holy Epic poem, attributed to Valmiki, which tells of the Life of King Râma (probably fourth century B.C.).

words, but with her right hand made the gesture that was usual to her when she beckoned her children. I understood. The special *mudra* sign-language, which imitates the attitudes and gestures of the statues of the gods, is used for subjects so holy that nothing from outside must debase them. My heart and Sakuntala's were in harmony. I knew that she would ask me to meditate with her at the first favourable opportunity, and so indeed she did, on the following morning as she crossed the inner court.

I followed her to the covered arbour at the end of the garden, where she seated herself after sprinkling a little water upon the ground from a vase. I sat down beside her.

'I know nothing,' she said, 'only how to say the Holy Name, which is also the name of the father of my sons.' She had no rosary, but with the thumb of her right hand she counted on the joints of her fingers as she repeated the invocations with their long and short syllables, to the rhythm of her breathing.

Sakuntala, with eyes closed and a serene expression, was living in the accomplishment of her *pathivrata-dharma,* that intimate act of worshipping the Bridegroom, who exists beyond the bounds of human love and the desires of heart and senses. I now saw her as the Mother-woman, the impersonal one, who is all self-discipline, austerity, penitence, who knows no discouragement nor any possible estrangement in her adoration of the Divine Bridegroom.

'I have no *sadhana* (spiritual rule),' she said one evening, 'not as you have, or Mataji, or the widow-aunts. I have only my *japa*, my repetition of the Holy Name.' That, for her, was a crystal lens through which she looked at the world and, until that moment, I had not understood the active part which she played as a wife, nor that she knowingly lived by a different rule from that of the other women. She had waited to tell me so until I asked her questions that were no longer prompted by mere curiosity.

Very early every morning when she awoke, Sakuntala traced a round spot between her eyebrows with a red powder. This sign means, to the enlightened consciousness, that a married woman is invested with the holy power of transmuting the "spirit-matter". Imprinted on a woman's forehead, it is the mark of divinity on the human plane.

Sakuntala's perceptions were very strong. She had been brought up from early childhood to be aware of the inner life, so that there was nothing mysterious for her in the myth of the immortal Sîtâ, of the Râmâyana,[1] who rose out of the bosom of the earth. For her, this happened every morning, when the Spirit covered the land and made it green again.

Her childhood had been carefee and happy. As the only daughter of her immediate family, she had simply waited for the day when her bridegroom would come. She had been chosen from among many other young girls to marry Vidyasagar Pandya, for in order to insure that his vast family should stretch far and wide and its sons enter into the politics and administration of their country, a bride was needed who would secure continuance of the family tradition from the very day of her arrival.

Sakuntala never asked herself why she should have been selected for that special task. It was her *dharma,* her way of fulfilling the Law. The way of love had been chosen for her. It would not emancipate, nor free her from other obligations, but it might lead her to inward freedom. This she knew. The lives of the uncloistered members of the family, those, for instance, of some of her girl-cousins who were far more independent and less tradition-bound, seemed to her simply "less near the centre". Everybody had his or her ideal, his or her personal form of worship.

'There,' said Sakuntala suddenly, 'that is finished! The Holy

[1] Princess Sîtâ was born from a clod of earth, while her father, King Janaka, was ploughing a field.

Name is my life. It is in my body, in my heart, and in my mind. It swells like a torrent, carrying everything before it. Then it becomes the Lord, himself, and everything grows blurred. The fires of the five sacrifices[1] which I offer rise very high . . .' She did not finish, but as we walked quickly back to the house, she continued to repeat with a look of rapture, 'Râm, Râm, Sîtâ-Râm . . .'

A few days later, I met one of Sakuntala's cousins, with whom I immediately became friendly. It was at her house that the women of the family assembled to listen to the temple-pandit, when he recited and expounded the texts of the Râmâ-yana and the Bhâgavatam.[2] Neighbours also came to profit by the pandit's wisdom and once a month brought offerings, which they laid in front of the great epic after bowing reverently. In this way, the pandit received six or eight rupees with which he bought wood, oil for his lamp, and tobacco. Mataji, herself, gave him a loin-cloth, rice, and melted butter.

'Unfortunately fewer and fewer women have time to come and hear the Râmâyana,' said Champa, 'and fewer good pandits nowadays expound it. The old ones die and their sons usually become postmen or minor officials. If one of them decides to follow in his father's footsteps he usually studies from books, instead of going to spend ten years at Hardwar to learn the meaning of its symbols from the mouth of a sadhu. A great deal of learning is needed to understand the Râmâyana,' she continued 'for the words have several meanings and convey ideas different. Take the word "wind", for example. It may mean the wind that blows through the forest, or the wind that accompanies Agni, the god of fire, and dries my sarîs when I spread them out over the hedge. But it may also mean my breath when I am talking to you, or *prâna,* the life force that fills our inward being. The reading of the "Holy Book" is a

[1] The five psychic centres of the body.
[2] A treatise attributed to Vopadeva (tenth-sixth century B.C.), which gives a detailed commentary of the life of Krishna.

help in understanding such things and in keeping them alive.'

It was nearly evening, and, as she spoke, Champa was play-ing with her little five-year-old son. I said, 'How do you pass these ideas on to your children?'

'When the sun sets,' she answered, 'the Scriptures say that something happens in our hearts, for that is when prakriti changes rhythm. Our bodies must then relax in order to help Nature, because we know things which our primitive selves do not. If you give a cow hay at such times she will not eat. She twists her head one way and another, and waits. Simple ignorant people light little lamps against the darkness at such times. The night outside and within themselves makes them fear. A flame, deliberately kindled overcomes Nature, for it is not her slave. I call my little boy. I make him sit down be-side me, and I say, "Shut your eyes, do not listen, try to feel nothing." That lasts for a moment and he gives me a wonder-ful smile. One day, in that moment of negation, he will feel the earth move and hear the Sound of Creation, like the music in a sea-shell. Then he will know that the beating of his heart is the same as that of prakriti in the Divine Consciousness.'

After a long silence, for I did not want to interrupt a time of perfect intimacy almost resembling meditation, we con-tinued to read an examination thesis, which Champa was pre-paring on the rights of women, a burning question now that they have been granted equal rights with men. She ended by saying, 'We women know perfectly well that we are prakriti, and that men still rule our social lives, but out of our very de-pendence we gather greater freedom of mind.'

11

Holi

YESTERDAY WAS THE LAST OF THE FOUR DAYS OF HOLI, which is carnival-time in the north of India. It is symbolic of the spring lights, and the lights of the Lord Krishna that appeared to the shepherds in the glades of Vrindavan. All barriers of caste are abolished, and at Shanti Bhavan the carnival-spirit was marked by the excitement of Anil and his younger brothers. Everyone wore old clothes, kept year after year for that purpose because they were stained and spotted with many-coloured dyes. One of the chief amusements is to squirt passers-by with brightly coloured water. They use brilliant powder-dyes, such as can be bought by the sackful in the bazaar. From a distance one might imagine oneself in the workshop of some painter-god.

On the first day I did not leave my room, but Holi came to me in the form of visitors armed with the coloured powder, which they threw into my face. There were congratulations, greetings with joined hands, and good wishes. Naraïn was the first to come, shy, awkward, slightly cringing, and even he had been made to look like a guy. Then came Panditji, Kumar, and the children shrieking like demons. On the second day, the women and little girls of the neighbourhood appeared, people whom I did not know and who did not belong to the family. They were far wilder than the men, and sprayed my face with powder until it looked like a Tibetan mask. I accepted the fun with good grace (it would have been wrong for me to take part in it) but after those first visits I put a padlock on my door.

On the fourth day, Panditji took me with a party of relations (all men, as usual) on to the terrace of the temple of
Nanda Devî, at the entrance to the town. This temple stands
like a fortress, jutting out over high rocks, with a carved
wooden look-out at the top. It has whitewashed stone walls
and a black slate pavement. There are no trees or flowers; it
gives an impression of the bleakness of that highland landscape.

This was the first time that I had entered the great doorway of the temple, under which some spectacular-looking
sannyasins had taken up a temporary abode, wearing robes of
ochre and red. With their matted hair done in a top-knot,
bushy beards, limbs rubbed with ashes, huge necklets of
rudrakshas (fruit-stones), and iron pikes, they presented a
terrifying appearance, in spite of their handsome faces and
child-like eyes. Panditji greeted them and, as he passed, murmured, 'Oh! the exaggeration and pageantry of India! Asceticism carried to extremes! Extravagant appearances, like ban-
yan trees or boa-constrictors! From what seas of wasteful
demonstrations of faith does the lotus flower of pure thought
emerge! We need no psycho-analysts here; everything is extro-
verted and shouted out loud. Do not apply your introverted
standards to us.'

A little farther on, a troop of actors, beating drums, were
the centre of a crowd. They were men of very low caste, with
dark skins and the sinewy legs of the underfed. They wore
gold-paper crowns, huge ear-rings, garlands of flowers, and
long, painted, horn finger-nails. Panditji knew them. We all
sat down, for the travelling actors had already seen us and
were coming forward, still doing their clever mime. One of
the boys, in female costume, was dancing seductively to the
Lord Krishna, with an ecstatic expression and lewd gestures.
He sang in a painfully realistic falsetto. Panditji gave them
some coins and a packet of the rice, which Kumar was carrying.

These actors came from a valley on the borders of Nepal. For more than an hour, Panditji, who was passionately interested in folk-lore and seized every opportunity to add to his collection of highland legends, told them stories from the life of the Lord Krishna, which they there and then mimed. 'How can such outcasts,' said he, 'whom no one ever tries to teach, learn the sacred texts? Their peasant lives are so far removed from the world of the gods whom they impersonate that one cannot imagine them succeeding. Yet all their movements are correct. Their instincts must lead them to understand a side of religion which we, Brahmans, have always denied to them. You can see how their own native intelligence, coupled with perseverance and loving care, has taught them to choose the appropriate gesture, to refine their voices, and subdue their passions. With such very simple movements they manage to express themselves fully, and reach a part of the Divine Essence which is especially theirs in the present century. And what do our sons do? They take the loves of the Lord Krishna to the cinema!'

Panditji was looking hard and bitter. He was expressing the Brahman's instinctive hatred of that progress which, even in India, threatens to destroy the old traditions. 'How stupid to say that India must give the younger generation "characters of steel",' he added. 'Our sons will grow up to be good officials, doctors, and politicians. They will give their wives refrigerators, and their farmers machinery; that is the fashion, but they will forget the relative unimportance of worldly things in comparison with the Higher Aims. One of these days, they will come begging for knowledge from those who still sing of the acts of Krishna with a full heart and perfect simplicity. At the present moment I believe that true knowledge is thrusting into new levels of consciousness. Evolution will be all the more stimulated by that.'

Later that evening, Ashok sent his servant to bring me some food prepared by his mother, whom I had not yet met.

The meal was exquisitely arranged and, to my huge surprise, included a dish of meat, which had simmered for hours in a wide-necked earthenware vessel. Naraïn proceeded to wait upon me with so much ceremony that I did not like to ask questions, but when I had finished, I pointed to the dish of meat and made an appreciative gesture. 'It is *prasad*[1] from the temple!' Naraïn said. 'Very rare! Only once a year!' Then I realized that I had been partaking of a ritual sacrifice.

On another of the days of Holi, there had been a three-sided conversation between Ashok, the Uncle-of-the-Gîtâ, and Panditji. We were all sitting on the terrace at the time, and the latter had been talking animatedly. Among much else, he had said, 'These days when everyone goes mad are a welcome rest for the awakened consciousness.' The Uncle-of-the-Gîtâ agreed. 'The noise of the crowd is not important; it is an excellent safety-valve and provides a rest from self-control. Nature, in a different way, has the same kind of truce. Once a year, for three days running, the earth is neither ploughed, raked, nor watered. It rests, it sleeps, and during that period of inactivity a process of involution occurs. Men understand this sleep, and respect a time when the Spirit, as it were, withdraws from the earth and the Creator contemplates his creation.'

'We know such things,' said Ashok, 'because we were taught them as little children, but in our personal lives something childish and violent always breaks out when Nature's river overflows its banks.'

At that point, Panditji suddenly seemed to realize my presence, for until then he had forgotten me. He turned and said, 'If you have been able to grasp something of the true silence that lies hidden beneath the madness of Holi, you will not have wasted your time.'

---

[1] Prasad: Food that has previously been offered to the gods, and thus sanctified.

12

Ashok

For some time past, my friendship with Ashok had been near to breaking point, and I could not succeed in improving my relations with him. The reason was simple. He had a most irritating habit of repeating everything that he said three times. It was his way. I tried not to let him see my exasperation, which increased whenever he persisted in saying 'Do you understand?' after the simplest remarks.

On this particular morning, when Ashok was talking of the Buddha, he said, 'The Buddha taught that all new ideas and all orders must be repeated three times if they are to be understood. That is absolutely true if you come to think of it! At the first hearing, a listener is passive, because he has not collected himself to grasp what is being said. What in him will grasp the new idea? At a second hearing, his mental machinery functions better, but as yet there is no trace of awakened consciousness in his personality to render him capable of registering what has been said and of making a reply. The third time, everything is different, for the personal part of the listener has been submerged and its place has been taken by "that" in him which understands. And that is what accepts or refuses. A choice is made. Something responds.'

'And supposing that I do not listen at the third time?'

'That will be because you do not wish to understand!'

Ashok was a perfect compendium of moral precepts, by means of which he had developed a personal rule reduced to the minimum of emotional and physical needs. He fulfilled his religious duties, did his work to the best of his ability, and obeyed his old mother implicitly. He went for long walks every day, plunged deep in his thoughts, sometimes taking me with him, either alone, or with Kumar. He believed that it was vital for him to have few friends and few possessions, so as to avoid complicating his life.

All that he knew about Western civilization he had learned from books, and from the young men's enthusiasm for the Western way of life once they had tasted independence, or their antagonism towards it when they defended tradition. Like the philosopher he was, Ashok watched the struggle of opposing influences from afar. 'You live in a time of crisis,' he would say, sticking his fingers into his waistcoat pockets. 'Take *Madame Bovary,* for example, the film which they are showing at all the cinemas. Do you really live like that? Fashions change, and so do means of communication, but the way in which people express their feelings remains the same. Your morality has been codified to such an extent that one can learn all about it by reading Jung or Adler, or any of the English text-books on sex or criminology.'

Ashok's mother was very old and had been an invalid for the past twenty years. She had always refused to consult a doctor, not so much from economy as because she accepted the ruination of her health as something ordained by God. 'Everything that God wills,' she said, 'is part of the plan by which the Creator and the created are bound together.' She had no mental problems.

'What will you do when your mother dies?' I said to Ashok.

'Everyone asks that question. I suppose that I shall marry.' He had already decided that when the time came, he would choose a woman of about thirty-five years old, one of those pioneers who serve their country and refuse to accept a marriage arranged by their families. There are not many such.

'It will be what you call a marriage of convenience,' said Ashok.

He had a servant who was entirely devoted to him. This man had, in his time, been a well-to-do peasant. That is to say, he had owned an allotment at the lower end of the valley, where the River Koshi flows northward. He had had a wife who according to the custom used to go out with a sickle to cut the tall grass for their cattle. They had been happy, until, suddenly, the gods dealt them blow after blow, removing first their son, then their daughter, then both of their cows. Even that was not enough. One day when the river was in flood, his wife, coming home late, had tried to cross it with a huge load of grass upon her head. Her husband, who had come to meet her, shouted 'Stop!', but she did not hear him, lost her footing and was carried away by the flood.

The poor man went mad with grief. For years he wandered about the district, refusing work and existing on charity. He would never spend more than two nights under the same roof, but went roaming on, wailing his songs of lamentation. Gradually, for some unknown reason, he grew into the habit of staying at Ashok's house and doing odd jobs, and did not run away when they spoke to him. At the end of five years, he seemed to have become a fixture. He worked intelligently, even cleverly, but would never accept money, preferring to live like a hanger-on of the family. He could often be persuaded to tell stories about the time when he had been a soldier, long before his peasant days. That part of his life was dead for him; he had entirely forgotten it.

This old man became attached to me, and whenever he brought a message from Ashok, he would let me give him four annas, which paid for his weekly allowance of tobacco. Ashok said, 'Be careful! You will find him coming every Monday!' 'Let him come', I answered, 'like an old uncle. He will simply be one more member of my new family.'

At that time I was studying Hindi from three sources, an

excellent grammar, by Scholberg, a vocabulary for English officers, full of *urdu* words, and a weekly review written in a rather precious style, closely resembling Sanskrit. Ashok watched my progress. The Hindi language has not yet been polished as Tagore polished Bengali, it is still the language of Tulsidas and Kabir, well suited for speaking of the heart and emotions, but not for political economy. Words for present day affairs are clumsy, and are used in passive constructions, not precise in their moods and tenses. Most foreigners in India use a very primitive form of speech.

Ashok sometimes saw me growing desperate at my studies. Then he would quote a text from the "Nîtis",[1] poems attributed to Châvrakya and designed for the education of young princes. It is written that "there are five things which a king can learn only by self-discipline and experience—the arts of loving his queen, of persevering in all things without ever losing patience, of husbanding energy in a long and arduous task, of recognizing wisdom in all its forms, and the art of accumulating true riches on every plane."

Ashok chose the following sentence for me to translate: "The only certain experience that should excite man's curiosity is the experience of death." 'But', he added, 'that is the one thing which man rejects.' When the grammar lessons thus strayed from the subject in hand, I had an opportunity of learning Ashok's thoughts. I might have adopted his point of view and altered my own ideas to match his, but each time I violently rebelled. He used to laugh at me, saying, 'Ah! so something is alive, after all, at the bottom of the deep rut which conventions have dug in you. But where is that something, the seed of your true being?'

One day he spoke to me of the "Amarakosha",[2] a Sanskrit

[1] Nîtis or "Practical Wisdom", a collection of moral rhymes (fourth century B.C.). The compiler is known by the name, Kautilya.

[2] The Amarakosha, or Nâmalinganushâsana, the oldest lexicon of Ancient India, of Buddhist origin (sixth or eighth century).

dictionary of rhyming tags which generation after generation of Brahmin children have learned by heart. He mentioned the name of some illness, and immediately followed this by singing several verses describing its symptoms, remedies, dangers, and the cosmic environment favourable to a cure. By following the instructions the disease is quelled. Unfortunately no one believes in the Amarakosha nowadays, and fewer people are cured!

When he was three years old, Ashok had begun learning to recite passages from it. His grandfather used to make him sit facing him and, for hours on end, would sing them with him, with modulations laid down thousands of years ago. As he grew older, he sometimes had an impression of coming across ideas in his reading which were so familiar that he felt he had always known them. It had become natural for him to inhale and exhale, breathing the ten names of Shiva, and to move his fingers thinking of the ten *Shaktis* (divine powers).

'Everything in the universe is included in the Amarakosha,' he explained, 'except the four things which the Sage forgot because he was using them at the time—his pen, ink, and paper, and the little carpet on which he sat. All the laws of prakriti are summarized therein in simple language. Thus men may learn to read the music of Nature, and accept even the discords and counterpoint which finally unite in the single resonance. The Amarakosha even provides the clue for escaping from Nature's clutches but in order to understand it one must know the language of numbers, for, in Nature, nothing is left to chance. Its laws divide the year into six seasons each of two months duration, and they teach men how to eat, dress, build their houses, think, and act. But the laws are often broken. He who brings disorder by disturbing the relationship between *Him who sees, That which is seen,* and *That which is,* is beyond the Law. That is rebellion,' added Ashok, 'and on the human level, such a man is outcast. On the level of the inner life, he is either perfect or accursed, or else on the road to becoming the one or the other. That is why every wandering sadhu is a living enigma. His Law is not our Law. May grace be his nourishment.'

We had been for a long walk and were sitting resting at the top of a hill, in a little wood full of flowering mimosa. Ashok said again, 'Yes, when a man has left the Law, he is either a saint or a pariah. In this connexion, I should like to tell you a story from the "Hitopadesha".[1]

'Two friends, as it might be ourselves, were chatting together. The younger said, "How is it that you are so just and honest in your way of thinking and acting?"

' "It comes from living among people who are full of faults and observing them without condemning," said the elder. "Remember this. The man who puts himself outside the Law has a right to do whatsoever he fancies. He is as free as one who is liberated in this life. This is how I learned that lesson. One day, as I was going to the village, I met a swâmi[2] in his saffron robe. He was holding a fish in his hand. I stopped him and said, 'Oh! reverend Sir, why have you got that fish?'

'My son', he answered, 'I am going to eat it! I sometimes also cook and eat beef!'

'Oh! reverend Sir, may the gods have mercy on you!'

'My son, when I am thirsty, I sometimes drink *bhang*.[3]

'Oh! reverend Sir, may the gods be with you!'

'My son, sometimes I go with women when I desire them.'

'Oh! reverend Sir, tell me, what rules do you obey?'

'My son, there are no rules for me. I am a lost man. I do as I please about all these things. But do not touch them yourself. Remember the golden rules.'

---

[1] The Hitopadesha: A popular Sanskrit book of moral tales, attributed to Vishnu-Sharman.

[2] A swâmi is a vegetarian and drinks no alcohol.

[3] An intoxicating drink made from hemp.

'Our actions reveal our feelings,
Our speech our ancestry,
Our children our integrity,
Our bodies that which we eat and drink,
Our expression our thoughts. . . .'

Ashok was silent for a moment. Then he said, 'There is truth in this story, for only by constantly increasing the sum of what is good can evil be diminished. But it is a matter for the individual to decide, for evil plays as important a part in life as good. The swâmi in the parable, with his fish, and his bhang, and his women, is just like myself, in my relationship as a lawyer with the judge, the accuser, and the accused, all of whom require my services. They are connected with one another only by a particular function. How can we possibly weigh these relationships, one against another. But stop thinking about it, or you will begin to have a false idea of things which in themselves have no real value.

'One of the most dramatic things that ever happened to me,' said Ashok, when he was talking about himself, 'was when my grandfather called me to recite before his assembled friends a page from that book, and another from Pânini's grammar. My voice was shaking and I looked round desperately for help. When I had finished, the guests put down the hookah, nodded their heads, and, turning to my grandfather, said, "You have been a good father to him." But as I went away, feeling much embarrassed, I thought to myself, "Why did they say that he has been a good father? He has not arranged a marriage for me yet. What kind of wife will he give me?" Now that my grandfather is dead, I am the head of a family and still unmarried.'

There was always something uncomfortable about my walks with Ashok because he went so fast that if I had not hurried we should have proceeded in single file like peasants, the man in front, the woman behind. In this part of India the mountain people take short quick steps, walking so that their heels hardly touch the ground. One soon learns to imitate them and to breathe from the upper part of the lungs in order to avoid puffing and blowing.

Today we passed the Christian cemetery, where some English and a few baptized Indians lie under the sign of the Cross. Very near them, beneath their protection, as it were, are one or two Chinese in sumptuous Buddhist tombs, although they are only poor exiled coolies who died in the bankrupt tea-gardens of that waterless region. It is a sad place, that cemetery which no one visits, and it seems discordant in a country, where life slips quietly along without emphasis on birth or death. The Hindus burn their dead on the banks of the River Koshi. How simple it all is! The funerals have no pomp, but from far away, re-echoing from one valley to the next, the monotonous chanting of

Râm nam satya haï (Rama is the Truth)
Satya bolo gatta haï (The spoken Truth is liberation)

marks the passage of a funeral procession, priest and bearers, a wooden litter with the corpse, wrapped, bound, and strewn with flowers. The men run, panting for breath. They pray fast and loud. Death passes at great speed. It is a long, straight, slippery path to the end of the valley. At night, from Shanti Bhavan, I could see the flames of the funeral pyres on the banks of the river, and the smoke mingling with the mists.

Today, we went to see the haunted house, which they call the "House on the Hill". It forms part of the estate of Shanti Bhavan and goes with about fifty acres of terraced land that was once well tilled. The house itself is a good one, with a roof of stone slabs that reminds one of a tortoise. But there is a *bhut,* a ghost, and no one yet has been able to dislodge it.

The bhut appears at night, sometimes headless and always obviously greatly troubled. It terrifies the people who see it.

When it vanishes, there is a gust of wind, branches are snapped and stones thrown. I asked who the ghost was, and was told that he was an unknown traveller who, many years ago, had been found lying with a battered skull in the snow before the house. Ever since then misfortune had befallen it. Nothing had prospered.

A stranger who did not believe in ghosts had once tried to turn it into a posting-house because it lay on the road between Kurmachala and Nepal, but forty of his mules had died within a few days. The last attempt to resuscitate it was made by two Europeans who tried to turn it into a Buddhist monastery. One monk had stayed in the house while the other went to meet their companions on the Tibetan frontier. He was never seen again. That happened several years ago, and now cacti have grown in the rooms between the stone flags and all the furniture is rotten. On one wall hangs a tarnished mirror, sole relic of what was once a comfortable house. The terraces have fallen in, and the fruit trees have run wild.

That was when the final chapter began, with a situation which all deplore but which no one has power to change. An old Mohammedan has settled into the house as caretaker, with a few goats and chickens. Every year, on the excuse of finding her a husband, he takes a very young Hindu girl from one of the families in the town, where children are many and food scarce. After a few months, he marries her off to a so-called "cousin" in the plains, and pockets her dowry. There is nothing to be done about it since he has the parents' consent, but the entire district is outraged by the scandal. These pariah children are willing to become Mohammedans in order to escape their misery. In other words, they are sold!

'The house is degenerating,' said Ashok. 'It is like a desecrated temple. Houses are like people, after death there is a period of disintegration until life begins again with the emergence of something new. Then someone appears, who unconsciously wipes out the mysterious *Karma*, because he has the quality necessary to make the change. Nature re-creates all such refuse; but it takes time.'

Ashok would not allow me to sit on the terrace or pick any of the splended daturas that grew in the abandoned garden. 'The breath of the bhut is everywhere,' he said rather crossly. 'It is like a thick fog; it smothers one. Let us go!' When we reached home, we neither of us told Panditji where we had been that day.

13

Prakriti, Nature and Woman

TODAY, PANDITJI AND ASHOK TOOK ME WITH THEM WHEN they visited some of their cousins, part of whose family lived all the year at Kurmachala. We went in order to meet another section of the family, whose home was in Rajputana, and who left there only during the university vacations. These cousins lived out in the country, where agrarian reform was a burning question, and their home was the tower of a castle, which had been built by the British on the ruins of a fortified wall. The rooms were vast. In that family, as in all the others which I had visited, I found a guard of honour drawn up to greet us, consisting of the younger Brahmins standing behind their elders. Very intelligent, well-bred, polite, and completely silent, they were introduced by their professional titles, Engineer to the Water Service, Assistant Veterinary Officer to the district, Assistant in the local Fuel Office, for all of them were budding civil servants. I found the usual disorder everywhere, the pleasant litter of educated men, piles of books, electric torches, rugs, attaché-cases, inkstands, and hookahs, all lying higgledy-piggledy without the least regard for tidiness. But everywhere I also found the scrupulous cleanliness of Brahmin homes.

The place where we were to sit was marked by a spotless white sheet, spread out on the well-washed flags of the terrace. Tea was served, and sweet biscuits, hastily purchased from a neighbouring confectioner, were offered on a banana-leaf with all the appropriate ritual. Around us moved servants, ill-clad as usual, but wearing fine, rich silk turbans.

Conversation centred around the coming marriages of Panditji's two nieces, one of whom was Uncle Biren's daughter. To my great surprise, I heard them openly discussing the choice between rival claimants for the hand of one of the girls. Professional matchmakers, astrologers, and priests had all sent reports on the two candidates. It seemed that the bridegroom had to belong to a family with the same number of quarterings as the bride and must be of the class of higher government officials, for that was the social level from which a new family must spring. Pandits, specially learned in Brahmin genealogies, were invited to the weddings, as well as many priests who followed the various cults of the five gods venerated in the three families.

The acharya whom I knew personally had come with us, and, at this point, he began talking vehemently about me, saying that he was not sure if I ought to be allowed to attend the betrothal ceremonies. I understood that two strictly orthodox female cousins were against it, which was why they were discussing the question.

What surprised me was that they should do so in my presence, but once again they were showing me the passive role which I must adopt, even when I was under discussion. I had already learned by experience that I should know only so much of the religious life of India as Panditji pleased to let me discover. For him, I was like Sakuntala, his wife, simply a field of prakriti, one aspect of ever-changing Nature, of which Woman is the symbol. In Her, the involuntary action of reproducing both mental and physical states of being is indefinitely perpetuated. I had submitted to being thought of as a "waste land" of prakriti, heavy *tamasic*[1] soil, where light only penetrates in stormy weather when the lightning strikes it. In *rajasic*[2] battles, when the elements rage and rain and wind batter upon it, a change sometimes occurs, a transmuta-

[1] *Tamas,* darkness, inertia.

[2] *Rajas,* action, power, violence.

tion into a new spiritual element. Like lightning in natural storms, heavenly fires, that is to say flashes of the Sublime Grace, are needed to penetrate the darkness of Primordial Matter.

All India, whatever degree of evolution her sons may have achieved, constantly feels a desire to turn to the Divine Mother, to Her, who is inconceivable, but is also the soil, virgin and transmutable, whose very dust is holy. "The soil is matter issuing from Brahman," say the ancient writings, "It may be changed first into air, then into spirit, and finally into consciousness."

I had seen Hindus returning from Europe, who prostrated themselves to embrace the soil of India, not out of patriotism as we understand the word, but because for them it was the pure humble vehicle of all possible transformations. It is the matrix from which seeds spring up; from which grows the tree of life, to whose branches all the birds of the air return to build their nests.

That is why I asked Panditji, when I felt the same longing, 'Shall I never learn to escape from the bondage of my body, those opposing impulses that alternate unceasingly— enthusiasm and doubt, love and indifference, humility and revolt. Shall I ever learn to go beyond?'

'Ah! If only I could promise that!' he answered. 'The Liberated prove that it is possible; they know the Truth and abide in it. But one must submit to great suffering before one can escape from this repetitive cycle. Fire from Heaven must strike long and deep into the soil from which such beings are evolved, in order to make them ever more refined, less and less earthbound. That fire is the purifying flame of tapas (austerity), gradually changing the densities of matter. The Shastras speak of bodies and garments of light.'

It was not always easy to submit to being waste land tilled by fire from Heaven, and at the same time to keep the sense of proportion which they seemed to expect.

A few days earlier, the Uncle-of-the-Gîtâ had told me a great deal about a fair that was being held in one of the neighbouring villages, famous for its musical clowns. I had said that I should like to see them and, immediately, he had offered to escort me. We had accordingly set out on the following day with Kumar, a bearer, food for a picnic, and a supply of drinking water, and arrived at the village about three o'clock in the afternoon. There we found great excitement everywhere, and at each street corner I discovered something new to interest me.

First, however, we went to the house of a Brahmin cousin, a lady who had invited other relatives to meet me. They welcomed me charmingly with garlands of flowers and much tea-drinking. There were recitations from the Sanskrit and classical dances by the children, followed by the Song of Râm-Nâm, with all the questions and responses chanted to the strange, reverberating rhythms that ordinarily thrilled me. On this occasion, however, I was exasperated by the length of the Râm-Nâm, probably because I was still thinking of the clowns. When I finally said good-bye to my hostess, I learned that they had already gone.

The uncle had tricked me, and I felt my temper rising but as ten people, including my hosts, were gazing at me, I could only smile (as many times I had seen Sakuntala smile), and thank them for their kind welcome.

We took the road back to Kurmachala, with torches of lighted pitch that crackled as they burned, giving the landscape a new appearance. A fortunate distraction for me! I walked along breathing rhythmically in time to my steps. The Uncle-of-the-Gîtâ and Kumar never ceased talking, until the former said, intending the remark for me, 'Some impressions should be avoided before they imprint themselves on one's mind, for they can be very hard to forget.'

Nothing more was said.

When we reached Shanti Bhavan, I thanked the uncle

politely but coolly and he left me, obviously feeling very much pleased with himself. We both knew exactly where we stood. He had courteously acceded to my wish to attend the fair, and at the same time had graciously done everything possible to prevent me from polluting my fields of thought and vision.

On this particular day, however, my whole interest had been centred on the young Brahmins in the house. Were they already married, I wondered, or would they accept a marriage arranged in the traditional manner, a choice in which they would not even be consulted?

I ventured to question one young man of about thirty years old. He wore a cardigan carefully buttoned over a flowing dhoti, and bowed when he spoke to me. 'During the period when the great mass of India is passing from the sensorial plane to that of consciousness, and until the best people are all fully engaged in the work that is necessary to the country's development, the equilibrium of India will continue to rest upon the women. Woman is the prototype of the Mother, who, in later years, instructs her sons in the cult of her *mantra*.[1] That first initiation is ten times more important for them than anything which a priest can give.' This singularly evasive answer was all that I could extract. I broke off the conversation so that the ensuing silence should be no barrier to our mutual understanding. When we left, I found that everything had been settled, except the propitious days and times for celebrating the weddings.

A few days later, towards the end of the afternoon, two of the young Brahmins came to pay me a visit. I hardly recognized them in their smart English clothes. One of them was the brother of one of the brides. He came to introduce her and to invite me to the wedding, and brought an invitation-card, stamped in gold. The bride herself, he said, was at that moment calling on Mataji.

---

[1] *Mantra:* Mystic phrase used in meditation.

It was Mataji who arranged the family marriages. She knew all the girls and boys of their caste and nothing escaped her eye. She knew every detail of the various acharas, the particular customs, obligations, and prerogatives of all the families that could be united by marriage. What is more, she had a reputation for being successful. What struck one most about her was her kindness and her modernity, all the more surprising since she could scarcely read or write, indeed, she had almost forgotten those arts because she had never needed to practise them. Her way of communicating with other people was to meet them face to face. Just as a blind man sometimes discovers from people's voices all the secrets that they would rather conceal, she had her own standards for judging the *samsaras,* the moods of depressions, worries, and impulses, in the minds and hearts of those surrounding her. When she had lived in the world, Mataji's life had been so difficult that she could understand and made allowance for circumstances. Nothing surprised her. With her great and fervent love of religion, she could absorb the sins of others. She "swallowed" evil, repeating "Shiva! Shiva!" the name of that all-powerful god, who swallowed the world's poison for its salvation and has had a blue throat ever since.

Mataji, with her wholly unsentimental way of life and her simple direct thinking, was always available. She had been a widow as long as anyone could remember, but although she never appeared at festivals or family ceremonies she was the very life and soul of the house. Everything was done through her. Panditji adored her; for him, she represented the perfect Mother, the Queen, the manifestation of the Divine in human life. Yet he was not her own son, for in Mataji's life, there had been a tragedy.

Panditji's father (whose name was repeated one hundred and eight times each morning by the chaplain) had married when he was past thirty, but he had had great misfortune, for his very young wife had died giving birth to his son. His relations had sent at once for another young girl, belonging to a strictly orthodox family, to replace the dead, and bring up the baby.

This second, seventeen-year-old bride was carefully chosen to keep green the memory of the first wife, but Panditji's father had died of a malignant fever only a few months after the wedding and she, herself, was left a widow. Her life was shattered. Mad with grief, taking the baby in her arms, she had hidden herself until she realized that she was doubly parent of the orphaned child, and must learn by self-denial and asceticism to win the respect of his large family. Her sense of responsibility, common sense, and practical religion had compelled them all to honour her.

The child became the great object of her love and found in her a perfect mother. She accepted without reserve or alleviation the harsh discipline to which widows were subjected at the beginning of the century. This rule laid down, among other restrictions, that she should prepare her own food and eat alone before sunset, always in her own home. Thus, even her movements were limited, and once, when after seventeen years she had had to return to her father's house to sign some deed, she had observed a strict fast during four days' absence.

For many a long day the family had seen her meditating morning and evening, her body rigid, the tears pouring down her cheeks, while her lips repeated the prayer of purification and her rosary slid between her fingers. Many years passed before the waves of her shattered longings became absorbed through the strength of yoga, and were transformed into clouds, which fell like refreshing rain on the ploughed furrows of prakriti. How did she learn to rejoice in "that which remains eternally empty"? how did she learn to drink at the well of knowledge? That remained her personal secret, but her life suddenly changed.

From that moment, religious asceticism became a pleasure. In her relationship with others and in her daily tasks, even with the child, everything was simple and well ordered. She withdrew still more, but now her face radiated happiness. They felt that she lived on spiritual food, for she said, 'In order to rise above prakriti one has to have the patience of a plant that exists on such humus as it can find, the concentration of a panther as it stalks its prey, the perseverance of a potter polishing an earthenware bowl until it shines like a mirror. The Grace of the Divine Mother dwells in such quiet tasks in the very heart of prakriti.'

Even with her clumsy manner of speaking, she made them understand that she had drunk at some indescribable source of life. Each member of the family was proud to venerate her, each envied her intensely active life. Naraïn said to me, 'Mataji speaks roughly, examines every grain of rice, gives out the clothes, scolds us severely, but when she crosses the court, no shadow follows her. That is where she is different,' which was another very Hindu way of saying that Mataji was much nearer to the Truth than the rest of us.

The fiancée appeared escorted by Anil. She was a tiny little creature and extremely shy. Keeping her eyes lowered, she bowed with signs of great respect and sat on the floor, facing me. There followed a long silence. Anil had gone, but the two students sat down with difficulty a little behind the girl, their smart trousers stretched to the utmost. I noticed the new shoes with rubber heels, which they had left outside my door, and the silk socks and ties, which had come from Italy. This Hindu-European medley seemed to me so comic that I had to smile, for there was I, wearing a sarî and shawl of raw silk, just as though I were a Hindu woman.

What, I wondered, did they expect of me? Ought I to put the bride through an examination? I knew that her dowry had taken the form of an expensive education under eminent professors. Had she attended lectures, or simply passed her examinations after careful cramming? On her finger, she was wearing a ring with a large precious stone, the gift of the fiancé whom she had glimpsed in Mataji's room. She knew that she was to live at New Delhi, in the same avenue as other officials, grade B, of the Finance Ministry. That was all she knew.

I allowed the silence to grow, although I knew that none of them would speak before I did, and that the girl would not raise her eyes. Every movement, the expression of her face, even her apparent humility, formed part of an explicit code of manners as familiar as the verses of a sacred chant, behind which lay concealed a thorough training in self-control. She was very beautiful, of the Aryan type, with a pale, colourless skin and a small diamond in her left nostril. On the day of her marriage, like all highland women, even the goddess Parvatî, she would wear a heavy gold nose-ring, with a cabochon ruby set in pearls.[1] Finally, I broke the silence, saying, 'I am very glad to be coming to your wedding. I am delighted to have this chance of knowing you better, all three of you.'

This changed the tone. The boys came forward, and the girl sprang to life. We began to talk of the problem of the meeting of East and West, which is so hard to bring about because each side always reacts according to its own traditions. One of the young men explained the difficulty by saying, 'Our grandfathers belonged to Queen Victoria's reign when Western customs were the fashion, and many members of our family went into the government service; but our fathers are of the generation that rebelled against anything coming from abroad. After they had acquired the culture, logic, and debating powers of the English, they passed down to us a strange, half-and-half state of mind, which prevents us from being consistent towards either of the inherited cultures.'

The other young man then spoke. 'The Mongolians forced our ancestors in Rajputana to escape to the Himalayas,' he said, 'but our fathers had no refuge from the Western ideas

[1] Village women still wear nose-rings, even when they work in the fields.

that intruded in the name of Progress. That penetration has so shattered the economic structure of our family life that no one can imagine the outcome. We used to live under an ideal form of communism, supported by our traditions. That has now been destroyed. The rules laying down the duties of each member of the family were stern, but they protected the freedom of the individual and defended the weak against the strong. Orphans were educated and married, for the rights of older members of the family entailed many obligations. The ideas of having separate banking accounts, and of equality among individuals—which, in any case, is impossible—have poisoned human relationships. My brother is a barrister; I am still only a clerk. At Aruna's wedding, in a few days time, our wives will wear different kinds of sarî, and we, different dhotis, to mark the difference in social standing. In the old days, Mataji would have given out the same sarîs and dhotis to everyone, and we should have been proud to wear them. That was true communism, accepted in order to obey a higher law; I have given you only one example.'

At that moment Panditji arrived in search of me. The conversation ceased. The three men sat down in a row, we women opposite them, and inevitably Panditji was the only one to speak. In three brief, respectful sentences they told him the gist of the discussion, and he then began to hold forth philosophically. 'It is really very simple,' he said. 'The West starts from the theory that everything has a beginning and an end, whereas we Orientals believe that life has neither beginning nor ending, but evolves cyclically, in a process of continual change. In that unceasing series of transformations we find our mental stability and our purpose in life. I know that Oriental and Western points of view are completely opposed; that is why it is so hard for us to understand one another, and why in practical affairs there occur so many mistakes and misrepresentations, so many cases of hurt pride, such a different appreciation of human values. Western scholars have discovered our sacred writings, arts, and traditions, but they judge them as inexact sciences by their own standards. They do not realize the changeableness of our conceptions, nor accept our attitude towards the fundamentals of life. None the less, for us, our own natural science of prakriti is an exact one. The Vedic *rishis* (sages) practised it in the past, but allowed only initiates to glimpse its essential principles. It will be for your generation,' added Panditji, 'to give a new interpretation of prakriti that will be understood in the atomic age. The mutability of forces, energies, and knowledge, no longer seems Utopian. We live in troubled times, but already one feels a reawakening of consciousness and, this time, Western philosophy comes half way to meet us.'

After a pause, he continued, 'What does Western materialism contain for us? It means not only a search after material benefits, but also attachment to certain intellectual forms and theories, and even to Christian philosophy, which has now passed into history and become a religion. For us, "History" is simply a certain period existing in time, and thus might suggest the false idea of beginnings and endings. Do you realize?' he said, turning to me, 'that Western logic has no truth for us? If you were to ask a Westerner to speak from the premise that time was nonexistent, and that there was a reality differing from his own conception, do you think that he could do so? He would probably find himself incapable, or else might feel as uncomfortable as we do, when we try to give permanent shape to what is either transitory, or has no reality except in the human mind. That is where we both stand.'

Panditji was in a good mood. 'The problem is with us even in this room,' he added, pointing his finger at me. 'You wear our dress, not only because it is comfortable when you sit on the floor, but also because it helps you to understand our way of thinking. And you', he said turning to the young men, 'create new responsibilities for yourselves by adopting foreign clothes and customs.'

I looked at the young bride, anxious to know what he would say about her. If I had not thus silently attracted his attention, he would have done nothing, but as he rose, he said, 'Woman, in her own person, is both the Divine Mother and prakriti, that is to say, she represents *yogamâyâ,* the union of prakriti and purusha, of matter and spirit. She it is who accomplishes everything. At the highest plane, she is symbolic of the universe (*virat*) in the eyes of her sons; at a lower level, she symbolizes the humblest types of labour and desires. She is mysterious, patient, the very temple of power!'

14

A Wedding

The wedding took place nine days later. A week earlier the marriage season had begun, and all day long the drums beat out a simple rhythm that became increasingly urgent towards nightfall, when it throbbed and flickered to the low, mournful accompaniment of bagpipes. The monotonous music continued day and night, for there was always some marriage being celebrated in one or other of the villages, near or distant, and the processions, headed by trumpets, flutes and oboes, passed the house one after another, on their way to fetch home the brides.

My terrace was a fine place from which to watch them and Naraïn an expert commentator. He knew from the tea-sellers of neighbouring villages, in whose booths the men sat gossiping for hours, all the details of all the local betrothals. With a knowing air, he weighed the merits of dowries and presents, being himself greatly favoured as a father because he had two sons and one daughter, which would mean two dowries received and only one to pay when the time came.

I was moved by the childlike simplicity of the first processions which I saw for I noticed nothing but the fancy-dress element, the bridegroom walking with difficulty in his lemon-yellow calico robe, a red shawl draped about his shoulders, his tiara of glass and tinsel, his cardboard mask,[1] and the umbrella tied to a pole, which a friend held over him. Around him went a few coolies bearing packages done up in red cloth, ragged musicians, their dust-coloured clothing sticking to their bodies, and the men of his village, who came as witnesses.

To Naraïn's eyes, the scene appeared very differently. He saw the Divine Bridegroom progressing in brocaded robe and scarf of fire, the jewelled crown upon his brow, and the mirror-encrusted parasol, emblem of royalty, that protects an august personage from the eyes of the curious. When the bridegroom came borne in a flower-decked litter or riding upon a mule, Naraïn was thrilled, for then he saw a prince with his retinue, or great captain surrounded by an army with shields and banners. To Naraïn, this deification of a shoddy hero was the cosmic force, which, at the temple, becomes Mâ Durgâ, the Divine Mother with the ten arms symbolizing her innumerable activities.

On the following morning, Naraïn would watch for the return of the procession bringing the bride to her new home, and would come to warn me. This time, the cortege had a different character. It was bigger, but at the same time less solemn and more human. It was headed by coolies carrying the bride's dowry, consisting often of a string mattress with embroidered counterpane and pillows, copper cauldrons and bowls, sacks of rice, and presents held on outstretched arms. Musicians walked in front of the palanquin, which was completely shrouded by a thick red woollen curtain, so that nothing could be seen of the girl herself. After her came the bridegroom in a litter or on foot, his mask lowered, chatting with his friends.

The time had now come for our family to play their part in the festivities, for the first of our two weddings was about to be celebrated. They were exactly like all the others, except

[1] The face of the bridegroom must not be seen because he appears in the character of a god.

in the length and magnificence of the processions and re-joicings. At Ananda Bhavan, the preparations were already finished. White lines had been scrawled on the treads of the stairs and a red flag flew over the entrance, with the word *Svagatam* (welcome) inscribed upon it in cotton wool and gold sequins. Strings of coloured electric-light bulbs adorned the roof and the trees on the terrace, while on the north side, where the reception of the bridegroom would take place, two women had just finished tracing the yantra of prosperity on the ground before the porch. This was the sacred diagram of the tree of life, which I had already seen on the family gotra. Three thrones had been set up, for the bridegroom, his acharya, and Uncle Biren.

Some relations were already arriving from the plains with their children, their servants loaded with rush baskets con-taining a variety of different objects, as well as bundles of pillows and quilted blankets. Naraïn, who had been promoted to the rank of major-domo, had a busy time of it. Nepalese coolies ran backwards and forwards between the house and the omnibus. Everything was done simply and cheerfully, without fuss, but with a good deal of suppressed excitement in the gestures, the hurrying to and fro, the arguments with coolies when the time came to tip them, and the latter's ob-jections, appeals, and, sometimes, yells of rage. Some of the guests were going to remain until after the second wedding, which was to be held four days later. All of them were near relations, and they were already making themselves completely at home. Hardly had the women entered the door before they had unpacked, washed their sarîs, and hung them out to dry over the walls and hedges. The smaller children, their eyelids blackened with kohl, were seized by the men and handed over to their mothers. The little girls wore wide satin skirts touch-ing the ground, and tight-fitting bodices. The small boys had silk turbans and gravely entered into the game of pretending to be grown up.

The first act of the marriage of Uncle Biren's daughter, Aruna, began at sunset. When Sakuntala and I arrived in our best silk saris, we were asked to go up to the bride's bedroom, but found that it was scarcely possible to reach it, for the house was full to bursting point. Every available space was already occupied. In the long low room, that ran the length of the corridor, a crowd of women were chanting Pahari folk-tunes to the accompaniment of cymbals. Farther on, in the bedrooms, trunks and bedding-rolls belonging to the guests were strewn about among accumulating piles of wedding-presents, all lying higgledy-piggledy. Children were taking the opportunity to play hide-and-seek, while their mothers arranged their hair and changed their sarîs. Incense was burning, prayers were being intoned. Standing apart from the rest, one aged and highly respected grandmamma, who knew the proper procedure better even than the priests, watched anxiously to see that every detail was correct. Four women, whose duty it was to act as bridesmaids at the moment of dedication, were getting ready to cover their rich wedding-sarîs with the rangvalî—the yellow cotton shawl stamped with patterns of red, which is the emblem of priestly authority.

Aruna was in the last room of all, looking quite serene, very much aware of her role as the "sacrificial victim" in the coming ceremony. Her hair hung loose on her shoulders, she wore no jewels. In her yellow cotton sarî, she had already ceased to belong to her old family. Her father, Uncle Biren, had bidden her farewell that morning during a pujâ, when he had adored her in the guise of Gaurî, the departing innocent, and had tied his last present to her left wrist, a few grains of rice and a silver coin done up in a red handkerchief. Then he had adored her in the guise of Mahesvarî, the mother that she would shortly be, and, finally, had asked her for her blessing. For the next thirty-six hours, until his dearly loved daughter had arrived safely in her new home, Uncle Biren would keep a strict fast.

When the sound of drums announced the arrival of the bridegroom's procession, the courtyard was filled with men and the porch with children, well-placed so that they could see everything that happened. The women watched from the upper windows. Guns were fired, torches were lighted.

Aruna was left alone, quite alone, waiting for the "gift" which her father was about to bestow on her, that unknown bridegroom, whose home was ready to receive her. I stayed by her for a little time and we exchanged gentle smiles. I pondered over this young woman who, in spite of her university education, was that day entering blindly into a marriage contract of whose meaning she was fully aware. How could she consent to lead a life governed by the Laws of Manu, a life in which her every action would have religious significance, which would mean sacrificing many transitory pleasures and the unfailing sublimation of every word and deed?

The moment seemed timeless. Aruna's calm and silence gave me a glimpse of that mystical period, so very long ago, when there had been a matriarchy in India, when Woman, through her close mysterious communion with God, was the Matrix, the Virgin bringing forth the Spirit—the eternal Virgin, who has given birth to the Saviours of mankind. That Woman the Aryan conqueror took to found his line. He enclosed her, veiled her, deprived her of her rights, but could never destroy her special power of communicating with God, a power fully recognized in the life of Brahmin families, for at the actual moment of a marriage, the sacramental act can be performed only by the mother of a family. The young bride of whom I have been speaking was prepared to oppose her allotted husband, if necessary in the cause of progress and for the sake of her country's evolution, but at the same time, she was determined to live her spiritual life in the deepest, truest sense, to maintain her mystical power, and fulfil her Woman's dharma (law).

I went to take my place with the other women looking

from the window. It was a fascinating scene. The bridegroom had descended from his satin-covered, gold-spangled litter, wearing a mask with long fringes, and was now receiving the courtesies due to his rank and position. The servants were placing in front of him presents of a blatantly untraditional nature, a portable typewriter, a pair of shoes, a solar topee, a walking-stick, an umbrella, etc. Uncle Biren dressed in a pale rose-coloured muslin turban bowed low to him, holding a tray with five candles, to the accompaniment of priests intoning prayers. The women and children were all gazing at an enchanting little girl of about ten years old, most superbly dressed, who sat at the feet of the bridegroom. She was the "ambassadress" who had come with him for the special purpose of welcoming the bride to her new family.

The actual moment for giving the Gift, or Kanyadan, is carefully fixed by the family astrologers. We had four more hours to wait, during which time there were entertainments in the inner court. Red carpets had been spread, a crowd from the neighbouring villages had assembled, and the staircases and the tops of the walls were packed with men, women, and children. I could see Ashok from my window, but he pretended not to see me. Seats of honour had been prepared for the bridegroom and his retinue, but the men were already collecting into groups; I had an impression that they all knew one another and were continuing the same arguments that they held every day at the Law Courts or in the corridors of one of the ministries in New Delhi. All this time, professional dancers, acrobats, jugglers, musicians, and snake-charmers were delighting the crowd.

The entertainments were still at their height when, after a light meal, the bridegroom, the little girl, the suite and the priests went into the Marriage-chamber, where a symbolical red curtain had been stretched across the room. I and the other women remained on the farther side. Aruna sat in the front row, her head bowed very low, completely enveloped in a sarî. Four women wearing the rangvalî, stood beside her, incognito, impenetrably veiled.

The verification of the titles of the two families, repeated by the two groups of acharyas, and the recitation of the names of all their united ancestors, took more than two hours. It was dreadfully hot, and I could hardly breathe. Outside the house, the wailing of the bagpipes succeeded the sound of flutes. The monotonous prayers were becoming exasperating, until fortunately the women behind me began to sing a popular Pahari song:

To find a kind husband for his daughter
   Her father has searched the four corners of the world!
   At last he has found him,
   The perfect bridegroom for whom he sought!

But his daughter is weeping;
   'Father, beloved,
   This husband does not please me.
   His skin is dark as night
   But I am pale as the lotus flower.'

'Darling, my daughter,
   Râma and Krishna are blue as the night,
   But your husband comes from the country of the light,
   Where I went out to seek him.'

But still the child weeps:
   'Father, beloved, take pity on me,
   Would you give me to this stranger?
   You may do with me as you please,
   I am a tethered lamb, I have no tongue,
   If you will it so, he can take me away . . .'

After the final rites, for a very brief moment, the mother of the family lifted the veil that covered the young bride, and the bridegroom looked at her in all her purity. Then the four bridesmaids surrounded her, clothing her with rich apparel given her by her father, and decking her with golden jewellery. When she had finally been enveloped in a red veil she was ready to be bestowed upon her husband.

Holding in her closed fist a gold coin and some grains of sesame and barley, the bride placed her hand in that of her father over a big copper tray. Only her thumb remained free, and that the bridegroom clasped while the Mother-head of the family, acting in her role as priestess, poured holy water over their three joined hands. Meanwhile, the priests recited the appropriate mantras. At that precise moment the red curtain fell.

The marriage had now been accomplished. Nothing remained but to clothe the bride afresh, on top of all her other garments, with a skirt of brocade and a veil woven with fine gold, her husband's wedding gifts, and to place in her nose the great gold ring hanging to the level of the chin. The rangvalî of her new family, presented by the little "ambassadress", ended by making her look like nothing but a bundle of veils wrapped one round another, the pinnacle being completed by a gold tiara.

It was a puzzle to imagine how Aruna managed to breathe under that heap of clothing. She certainly could not have moved without assistance and was accordingly led, pushed, and dragged through the remaining ceremonies that lasted throughout the night, bound to her bridegroom with a yellow scarf. There was a service of adoration, pujâ, vows exchanged while walking seven times round a fire, symbolizing sacrifice, ritual in which only girls younger than herself took part, and in all of these rites, she was the central figure.

Then a plaintive song was sung, expressing the bride's weariness and fears:

'Today I am like a fledgling on a branch,
But tomorrow I shall fly away.
Father!, call for bearers,
Let them prepare my litter,
For I must begone . . .
My heart is heavy with grief,
For I have become a stranger
In the home where I so often played.
Barriers have arisen between us,
Mountains and rivers already separate us.
Oh! Father!, why have you given me away . . . ?'

I do not think that the young bride had more than two hours' sleep that night, for early next morning, even before dawn, the musicians had begun to salute her, and the priests soon after started their pujâs, presided over by the bride and bridegroom, still symbolically bound together and weighed down by their ceremonial dress, their exhaustion, and the sadness of their farewells.

When I arrived with Sakuntala and Protima, some relations were already leaving, each carrying a coconut, a present from the bridegroom. All were in tears. When it came to my turn to say goodbye, I went up to give my good wishes and my token-present, a brightly polished silver rupee. The bridal couple were ready to depart. For the last time they stood together like icons on the threshold of the house, their crowns giving them height, their features motionless, their movements hieratic. At each repeated gesture bidding farewell to her old family, the bride seemed to become more dejected, but she managed to hold back her tears. Her palanquin was waiting. She stepped into it and the heavy red curtain fell around her. Then her husband lowered his mask and entered his gilded litter. The procession set forth, headed by drums and fifes, in all its traditional splendour.

I wondered what would happen next. Protima gave me

some idea when she described her own wedding to me: '. . . then I was able to cry. And then I was so tired that I fell asleep. I was fifteen. It is best to marry young, it is so much easier! When the palanquin stopped, I was terrified. My husband took me by the hand. I walked forward, but I could see nothing through the thickness of the veils until he said, "Here is my mother." Then I prostrated myself. They covered me with one more veil before letting me cross the threshold. It was in front of the tutelary gods, when I had paid tribute to them in the presence of the women of the family, that my husband's mother took off the ceremonial veils, removed my crown, lifted the gold veil that hung lower than my chin and, last of all, the red veil. My face was all swollen with crying, my hair was matted, my nose enormous, but Mataji took me in her arms. There were still many other ceremonies to be gone through, and then, on the fourth day, the little red bag on my arm and the one on my husband's were taken off, and our married life began.'

15

An Eclipse and a Fair

LAST MONTH THERE WAS AN ECLIPSE OF THE SUN. THE entire life of the household was upset by it and I think that other houses in the neighbourhood were equally disorganized, for the sound of conch-shells never ceased. The young itinerant priests worked as hard as water-carriers, rushing from house to house with trays loaded with offerings, muttering hurried blessings. Even a little dumb priest from one of the mountain-temples found a congregation. He was a piteous sight, with his wild gestures and tearful eyes. When I paid him two annas, he put sandal-wood paste on my forehead and gave me a few flowers from his shrine. On such unlucky days everyone does his best to placate the priests and gain their goodwill.

Eclipses of all kinds are difficult periods on the psychological plane, for the forces of nature are in opposition and no one can foresee the consequences. Here they believe that a lunar eclipse is always disastrous because the moon is the symbol of spiritual truth. When the sun swallows her up, the soul is momentarily ejected from its abiding place, with resulting disquiet on every plane of consciousness. It is considered a tragedy that there should be three times as many eclipses of the moon as of the sun.

During a solar eclipse, like the one that occurred last month, everything is different. Mistress of the sky, the moon sails in front of the sun and proclaims her victory. Nevertheless, it is dangerous, because her fiery antagonist is very strong and her victory is seldom complete. That is why men hide their faces during an eclipse and those who in either an actual or metaphorical sense possess a cave, withdraw there and meditate. Only little boys, who are not yet initiated into the Brahmin religion, are allowed to watch through smoked glasses. Even Anil was stopped by Kumar when he tried to join them.

Not one of the women was to be seen. They had all assembled in Mataji's room to say the appropriate prayers and to meditate. They held their babies on their laps or laid them on the ground on folded sheets. No one watched the sky. The atmosphere in the house was oppressive. Before going to join the other women, I went to say good-morning to Panditji in his study, where he was fasting with so little fuss that one would never have realized it if one had not known. He did no work, and none was done in the bazaar, the law-courts, the banks, or the post-offices. No leases were signed on that day, nor any other legal contracts in all orthodox India. No fires were lit within the houses, no one paid visits. This abstention bore a direct relationship to the behaviour of the two celestial bodies. 'The world above and the world below', explained Panditji, 'compel our attention during an eclipse. We are witnesses of an encounter between two great powers. What is our position, we wonder, with regard to these vast forces? In the ordinary way, we behave like puppies quarreling over a bone. Greedy, thoughtless, tumbling one over another, we are apt to forget our dependence. An eclipse serves as a reminder.'

All that morning, everyone connected with the kitchen had been subjected to a stream of orders from Naraïn. Every black earthenware water or cooking pot had been carefully broken, and already the potters were waiting in front of the house-doors with netfuls of new ones to take their place. All the food that was still remaining in the house was thrown to the cows and goats, the curdled milk was poured into the gutters for stray cats. Copper pots were rubbed and polished with ashes, the court was sprayed with water and swept with dried cow-dung. Only the butter-pots, hanging in their nets from the kitchen rafters were spared, because they had been well sealed with wooden stoppers.

When the eclipse was over and the good, clear daylight had returned, conch-shells in every temple of the town sounded together. The children had clearly been waiting for this signal to give vent to a chorus of shrieks and yells, and no doubt the crows, too, were ready to join in. I saw men and boys come out of all the houses, armed with sticks, and go off along the roads in little groups, beating a tremendous tattoo on old tin cans. Where they managed to discover such an enormous number of ancient petrol cans and old jam-tins I could not imagine. Anything served for the purpose of frightening the sky-devils, especially this tinkettle racket, these staccato, complicated rhythms.

Yesterday was the day of the local fair at Kurmachala, which coincided with the commemoration of the marriage of Shiva and Parvatî, which, according to tradition originally took place in the temple of a neighbouring village. The women had watered corn to make it sprout for the occasion and stuck a little bunch under the head-dresses of their husbands and sons. The men went about all day with sprigs of wheat under their turbans or black caps.

Mataji had baked and roughly coloured two little clay figures, and had given them to the priest to put upon the family altar on a carpet of flower-petals—jasmine, zinnias, and pinks, arranged in a pattern. Shiva and Parvatî enthroned, decked out in satin robes, crowned with tiaras of gold wire and glass beads, looked like some great Lord and Lady, come to pay a visit. We brought them tribute of the first-fruits of the fields, fruit, perfumes, and pieces of money, all offered with the most reverent devotion. 'Until this pujâ ends grant us that you will dwell in these humble forms,' was the prayer of the family chaplain. In the kitchen, dishes had been prepared of fried rolls filled with the most unexpected mixtures, white cheese and ginger, apricot pulp stuffed with spices, sugar cane and bananas. I was given my share of these good things, but alone in my room.

When evening came, Mataji prepared to place the little figures, now void of divine power, in the courtyard where the night dew would dissolve them. Panditji noticed the sadness that always comes over me when the image of a god is destroyed after fulfilling its purpose as an aid to worship. I always find it hard to discard a "form", no matter how humble. On this occasion, he intervened. 'Would you care to keep them in your room?' he asked. 'Would you be capable of paying continual homage to them in your mind, your heart, your every bodily action? It is a serious matter.' I fully realized that he was not joking, for more than once he had spoken to me of the method of endowing a worshipped image with Divine Power (Shakti), and the absolute necessity, once the service of adoration was finished, of freeing that power from the figure of straw or clay that had been its temporary home. Until a form is completely dissolved, it will always contain something of the Presence that dwelled therein.

Panditji looked me straight in the eyes and held my gaze. Something in me urged, "Go on, accept! this would be a new experience"; but with another part of my nature, I respected the religion of my hosts far too much to serve them ill. 'No!' I answered. 'I should not be able to do that!' Panditji laughed. 'Tomorrow', he said, 'you will see how little is left of them!' and Naraïn directed a stream of water on the two small figures lying against the outside wall of the courtyard. Next morning nothing remained but the twists of straw that had once been the backbones of the gods.

No rain fell, and underlying the bustle of the fair was deep foreboding about the local crops. The monsoon was already three weeks late, although the relief of one violent storm had

given us false hopes. The crows in their hundreds were holding a parliament and cawing in the pine-trees on the hill, but
Indra, King of the gods, was unmoved, hidden, as he was, by a
veil of dust beneath a stifling sky in which no clouds could
be seen.

Naraïn returned home for a few days, accompanied by two
of the uncles who had gone to live in his village for the time
being. The cows are already being fed on human food; but
what the beasts eat now the people will need later, for famine
threatens, although many peasants have a store of useless
rupees. Everyone is anxious and depressed. The fields are
green, but a light wind is blowing that will parch the corn if
the rains do not come. The people do not grumble, they resign
themselves to dying of hunger, just as they will forget their
cares if relief comes. No one rails against God. He moves like
a child, supremely illogical, obeying no known Law. He, alone,
fulfils no Law and is responsible to no one. What He is, He is.
He creates. That is why exquisitely beautiful and horrible
things exist together in a many-toned harmony, containing
discordant notes that cause us deep disquiet. We know so little.
The peasant does what he must and praises His holy Name.
If the rains come he will live, if they fail he will die. God is
in the rains that come. God is in the rain that stays away.

This is what Naraïn explained to me on the morning when
he brought my tea before leaving. His wife and his three children were living in the village but he did not complain. The
only change at Shanti Bhavan was that the music of the flutes
was replaced by the wind sighing, like waves in the top of the
pine-trees.

16

A New Chapter Begins

The temple, which we went to see on the day of which I am now speaking, stands at the top of a small isolated hill, reputedly the scene of many legends. The district is connected with the Chand dynasty (feudal princes of olden days), and local legends tell of boons conferred by them, of intermarriages between valleys, of blinded ambassadors, and the massacre and mutilation of slaves. It is a harsh landscape, and the burning sun eats into the stones. There are no flowers, only the loud chirping of grasshoppers under the noonday sun.

Our first stop was at the house of the blind music-teacher, whom I already knew, a man with the clear-cut features and long sensitive hands of the miniatures of Rajputana. He was sitting upon a rush mat when we arrived, teaching a class of ten little girls to sing classical scales, and accompanying their voices on his vina. He stopped the lesson; the little girls prostrated themselves before us, and sang the "Worship of the Guru", the hymn that is chanted in every house before daybreak. Then they fluttered away like a flock of butterflies, their anklets tinkling gaily. The blind man's room was very dark, for the straw blinds had been pulled down. There was a clothes line with his washing suspended from it, and musical instruments upon the wall. The effect was one of poverty enlightened by the presence of God. The sun burned our faces when we stepped out-of-doors.

Our next visit was to a house, facing south, in one of the outlying parts of the town, in a quarter for those of inferior caste (*shudras*). The mistress, a youngish woman with a croaking voice, received us on the terrace with her four children. She taught drawing and domestic science at the school. It was obvious that she had heard about me, but was not expecting me that morning. She had another visitor, a Mohammedan schoolmaster, known by the name of Ali Khan, and, almost immediately, we three, the Mohammedan, the Shudra woman, and I, the foreigner, united to form a common front against Panditji. What was he, a high-caste Brahmin, doing in that strange company? Was he simply trying to satisfy his desire for liberalism? Would he, I wondered, accept the cup of tea which they offered? I saw him shudder almost imperceptibly, but he took the cup and drank.

'Why I come here,' he said almost casually, 'is to talk of something that is of common interest to us all. I mean immortality, the quest of wise men since time immemorial, the sole aim of this life. You three may argue the matter interminably, but we Hindus live in the certain knowledge of "perpetual change"; we love God unreasoningly, we adore the Divine Mother without asking why, because our very lives are deduced from the existence of God. On the day when we can re-unite everything with primordial life we are saved, for that is God, Himself. The family presents the environment through which Divine Power best finds its way. There it can work, penetrating gradually into our minds, hearts, bodies, and blood, until the dead centre is reached, after which, the current gradually rises until the blood beats to the rhythm of creation, until the whole body sounds the call, until the heart utters the Holy Name, and the mind bends the will to obey the Law. Then something occurs that is beyond death and the endless reduplications of the world. Everything is contained in that Divine Force of Shakti, that energy that interconnects the descending and ascending spirals of Divine Power. That same Force is resident in the temple on the hill, to which we are now going. Would you like to come?'

'I will come as far as the door,' said Ali Khan. He was plainly irritated by our desire to visit idols made of stone, and did indeed leave us when we reached the temple. Panditji rang a bell, and an ancient acharya, reputedly a centenarian, opened to us. He was bent almost double, but held a staff, which he twirled about his head when he wanted to drive away those to whom he refused admittance. As caretaker of a temple of formal worship, he was guardian of the "imprisoned" power. 'Shanti! (Peace!),' said Panditji, pointing to me. 'She comes from the other side of the water, but she belongs to us. Today it is I who am impure. Let me have water!'

Panditji rinsed his throat, washed his face, hands, and feet, and threw a few coins to the servant of the aged priest, who was furiously angry at my presence but could do nothing about it, since Panditji had a right to bring me. Several small temples, ill-matched and very commonplace-looking, were distributed between the trees at the top of the hill. Panditji led me towards one of them. 'I should like it', he said, 'if you would place your forehead upon the stone step, before the *point,* which, in the abstract sense, serves to indicate the ideal centre of the universe. You will always remember that action. The symbol is universal, but here it is a living sign, because millions of people for thousands of years have come to this spot to make that particular gesture. Henceforward, you will have the rest of your days in which to discover that same fixed point in yourself, that base of the vertical "axis of life", around which circulate all the actions of your inner life. Your life will then find its proper means of expression. You will live in that secret power without ever mentioning it. I know no more than that, but later, at a suitable moment, someone else will come to guide you. . . .'

Panditji's instinctive emotion communicated itself to me, although he restrained himself. I placed my forehead on the clumsily carved step of the little temple before which we were standing. It was a windswept chapel, with a round stone emerging from the centre. The temple itself stood in the midst of a vast circle of mountains, just as, symbolically, it was the centre of meditations that led towards the plane of supreme wisdom (buddhi), which Panditji described as being beyond anything that we could imagine, except by a process of negation ennumerating all that buddhi was not. 'In order to arrive at such wisdom,' said Panditji, 'you have to start from some concrete example and, by making an effort of consciousness, rise above the planes of ordinary existence. Vines also need a prop round which to twine themselves. Even the most ignorant Hindu knows that much, and according to his capacity devotes his life to that kind of study. However poor he may be, he is always the disciple of a guru, and the guide of someone less aware than himself. It is everywhere a question of hierarchy.'

'Where does love come into all this?' I said.

'Love is a relationship set up between two different planes, between two states of consciousness, between two individuals. India is like a huge test-tube, in which all our religious efforts become condensed and distilled by some means or another. Drums, cymbals, conch-shells, prayers, incantations, raptures, are as much part of the rhythm of India as is silent meditation. For India is clamorous, and agitated, as well as infinitely patient, as the seasons of her life succeed one another.'

We came down almost running from the temple, our mouths full of mandarines which the priest had given us, and made a long detour to the forest half way down the slope. We wanted to see the scattered ruins of some Buddhist monasteries (viharas), dumb witnesses of persecutions that have pushed Buddhism back beyond the borders of Tibet.[1] Legend has it that the goddess Mani Joginî six times released violent tem-

---

[1] These struggles are dated approximately to the ninth century. Srî Shankaracharya, the greatest of the Vedist philosophers, created the ten Dashnâmi monastic orders, and purged Hinduism by fighting Buddhism, Jaïnism and Samkhya.

pests that prevented the sacking of such monasteries and con-
vents. On the seventh occasion, eighty-four thousand sacred
books were destroyed by fire, and the monks and nuns were
forced to fly or sacrifice themselves to the gods. Srî Shankaracharya finally cleared the region of Buddhism, with the
help of well-armed princes. Then came the all-pervading jungle, and later, the King of Nepal's conquests of the highland
valleys again changed the nature of the countryside. History
is vague and legendary. None the less, the gods continued to
dwell in these temples until the last of their priests abandoned
them. Panditji thought that ten generations of shepherds and
woodcutters had thereafter brought offerings. Miracles still
continue there showing that Divine Power is perennial.

We had to climb and use our electric torches in order to
find the altar, made out of the rock with stones of different
thicknesses, and carved to represent Shiva and his wife Shakti.
The ornamentation had been newly painted. An offering of
flowers and rice-grains had been placed there quite lately, and,
outside, we came upon an old woman meditating under a tree,
her sarî wound round her like a shroud.

Earlier in my visit, Panditji had taken me to another temple,
where miracles are a commonplace occurrence, judging by the
number of ex-voto offerings, in the shape of bells of all sizes,
that hung suspended in garlands from the roof. This temple
was built in the sixteenth century, and had been smartened up
with an overhanging roof of corrugated iron. It was the shrine
of a local god, whose name had been corrupted to "Galla". He
has considerable influence even at the present day, for, according to Panditji, he still acts as arbitrator in the decisions of the
local court of justice. There is never a lawsuit among the coun-
try-people but they bring him proof of their rights and promise him offerings before putting the case into the hands of a
lawyer. This god, in his earthly life, was a rajah, vilely mur-
dered by his relations out of jealousy of his flocks and herds.
He is the defender of the weak. They say, that many centuries

ago, he saved members of shudras from the encroachments and tyranny of the Brahmans, and has punished wicked judges through their posterity for many generations. He is regularly offered sacrifices of goats, to appease his anger.

In such conversations, Panditji was apt to pass from purely abstract ideas to the simplest native customs, just as he talked volubly about the delicate machinery of the nerve-centres in the brain, and in the same breath of the often crude work of men's hands, gathering all these matters into the greater unity of the whole body of India. 'Do not meddle with our life,' he once said to me, 'do not dissect it either in love or dislike. Try simply to absorb the essence of it, so that you may better understand your own inward evolution, which is trying its way through nature's jungle.'

'Why should India conceal her technique for meditation?'

'India conceals nothing. This is not something which one can learn; it is something that must be lived. You are in too much of a hurry. India's rhythm is as slow as an ox-cart on the earthly plane, but you would like it to be as quick as lightning. Both are right for their functions, like the fingers on a hand and the nerve cells in the brain. To make ourselves remember, to make this idea more real to us, we Brahmans, who read the Vedas, put dust upon our tongues so that we may know its taste. Peasants, who live far removed from the Vedas make the opposite gesture; joining their hands above their heads, they gaze at the sun, repeating the Names of the gods. Both gestures are links in the great chain of life, and indispensable in their respective places. They are spiritual nourishment for beginners, and bodily food for those on a higher plane of development. From the True Self, to the dust of the earth, all is holy. Even the dust forms part of the universal plan.'

Panditji turned towards me: 'Would you be capable of eating dust without being afraid of catching typhus?'

'No,' I answered, 'and certainly not now that you have

mentioned it. But I will eat dust if it is a sacramental act in the communion with Nature.'

Two days later, I learned from Naraïn that a sadhu was staying at Shanti Bhavan. He was living in the garden-house that could be reached without crossing the inner court. He had come up from the plains and was returning to his hermitage before the monsoons began. I discovered no more about him until that evening, when Panditji said, 'Srî Satyakama is here; he leaves tomorrow morning.'

'Who is he?' I asked.

'He is a scholar engaged in translating the Vedas. He has childlike simplicity, and lives a long way away, up in the mountains.'

'May I ask for his darshan (blessing)?'

'I am going to him this evening at six o'clock. Why do you not come with me?'

I was ready at the appointed time. We left our sandals at the door of the little house, where we found Srî Satyakama standing to receive us. I noticed his gentle laughing eyes, his delicate features, and small beard. He was wearing a sannyasin's cap and ochre robe. Panditji said, 'This is she,' making a gesture towards me. We bowed to one another with joined hands.

A carpet had been spread on the veranda and we sat down, the men with their backs to the house-wall and I against the wooden balustrade. I expected that Panditji would say something, but nothing occurred. A strange silence fell upon us, enveloping us completely. Surrounding objects stood out in higher relief, for instance, I noticed a bunch of grapes hanging from the vine-trellis. "That", I thought, "will never ripen before the monsoon." Two ladybirds were trying hard to climb the same post of the balustrade, and then climbed down again without pausing. I watched them idly, and as I did so felt that Srî Satyakama was gazing intently at me. I looked up, but he, too, was watching the ladybirds.

Shortly afterwards, the silence became so oppressive that it seemed to weigh upon my shoulders like a cloak. I had an unpleasant impression of time without end. Then came a change. I felt I no longer knew what I was doing; I yearned to escape. My back and neck grew numb. Objects about me took on unnecessary importance, for instance, I noticed with displeasure a loose paving-stone, a broken window-pane, whitewash flaking off the wall. Should I be able to bear it much longer?

Then the atmosphere seemed to lighten and, at the same time, there came relaxation of mind and muscles, a slackening of tension in the plants and trees, in the very air itself. My breathing became almost imperceptible, my body felt supple, as light as a feather; I thought that it was filled with a new consciousness that came from the heart.

Two or three hours passed in this way. Night came with the stars and the crickets. At a certain moment, I saw Panditji bow before Srî Satyakama, who placed his hand upon his head. I did the same in bidding him farewell, and I, too, felt his hands upon my head. We left him without breaking the silence. The only noise was the gentle sound of our sandals on the gravel path. Srî Satyakama remained seated.

As we neared the house, Panditji was suddenly overcome by a choking fit, such as seems only to afflict Hindus. Air whistled in his throat, and he gasped for breath in an agony, his whole body was subjected to a violent upheaval. The house door slammed behind him.

I did not see Srî Satyakama again at that time, but I wrote to him, and he answered as though he had known me for twenty years. "I know", he said, "that I can help you to become aware of what you have inwardly discovered. I suggest that you should spend the monsoon months alone with yourself. Sannyasins stop being itinerant during the rainy season. They settle down somewhere and live their renunciation in complete solitude.

"You must not think that those who answer the call are

free. They take the road and, at first, that is all that they can do. All the rules which they have followed have become part of them. They are within. All the new austerities to which they long to submit wait for them in the solitude which they must learn to conquer. Sannyasins follow the rule of never remaining under any roof for more than three nights. When you walk through the forests of the Himalayas you come across heaps of stones that mark the way of great rishis, who, thousands of years ago, left their homes for unknown destinations, crook in hand and in their hearts the quest for the Divine Essence. You must take a stone and add it to the pile, bearing fresh witness. You must say, 'Protect me'. Each movement towards liberation is a struggle against the weaknesses and opposing impulses of our natures, until there comes a time when, by willing obedience, you find yourself gradually submitting to the Law of the dharma that leads to higher levels of consciousness. It is all a question of solidity and rarefaction."

I wrote a bad answer, because I did not understand him; but his next letter paid no attention to that. "If you decide to come, you will be welcome. You may count on me. Now we must think of the practical side because we must both be wholly independent. I am no one's guru. I have nothing to teach. I have rice, corn, and charcoal enough for the summer months. Bring some paraffin and your own lamp. That will be enough." He had added a postscript. "Buy yourself an extra lamp-glass; there are no shops on this mountain. A peasant comes regularly to bring milk and potatoes."

I immediately decided to go. Panditji was a great help. He himself had to appear at an inquest on the other side of Sonepur, the town nearest to Srî Satyakama's hermitage, and he offered to make a detour in order to accompany me. Nothing more remained to settle except the day of our departure.

17

The Great Forest

WE SHOULD HAVE LEFT TWO DAYS EARLIER, BUT OUR start was unexpectedly delayed. Why, I could not imagine. Our caravan had been ready for more than a week, and all the provisions were packed. None the less, it seemed that we might not leave for another forty-eight hours. 'One never starts a journey on a Tuesday or a Saturday,' said Naraïn, 'for those are the days of Devî, the Divine Mother.'

'What would happen if we left on one of Her days?' I asked.

'Hm! There might be a black panther in the way, or a bridge might break, or perhaps bandits. The forest is huge, people do manage to get lost.' When Naraïn spoke of death, it was always in images. 'One big hiccup and it is all over,' was one of his sayings.

I let them see my impatience to be off, probably because of Sakuntala, to whom I had already said goodbye. My room was empty; all my books were packed. I had nothing to do but wait, camping out among my belongings. Panditji merely shrugged his shoulders. 'Why should the delay affect you?' he said. 'You are going from a Hindu home to the retreat of a Hindu teacher! He will understand. In any case, there is nothing to explain. You could not travel alone.'

Our party consisted of Panditji, myself, a sadhu who was travelling in the same direction for the first three days, two of Panditji's chelas (two young pupils of his, who were about to enter politics on the side of his party), two servants to cook our meals, and two coolies to carry the bedding-rolls and provisions. We were taking saucepans, charcoal, clarified butter, rice, flour, spices, and condiments, as well as a supply of drinking-water. I had stretched the rule by adding a tin of Nescafé and some chocolate; on long journeys one can never be sure of meals being punctual or comfortable.

Indeed, travelling, as we were, at the beginning of the monsoon season, we ran the risk of meeting violent storms, which might be very dangerous, for clouds come down upon the mountains and the way is easily lost. When the storms are over, however, one sometimes catches a glimpse of ranges of snow mountains twenty thousand feet high, or more, that cover the entire horizon with their white summits.

We set out eventually on a Friday morning, five days later than intended, after Mataji had properly blessed and bestowed offerings upon us. The whole of the first day was spent in extricating ourselves from the deforestated areas on the Kumaon mountains, whose trees had been used in the last century to provide sleepers for all the railways of India. Such deforestation has proved a criminal folly, for it has led to soil erosion and the drying up of streams, since the icy burning winds of Tibet now blow across bare ridges. From time to time, in that empty landscape, we saw a white dot that was the temple of a goddess. Finally, we reached the beginning of the forest itself, looking very ugly on its approaches because great limbs had been lopped off, or blown down by fierce winds. The path became more and more difficult to follow, the last of the houses disappeared behind us, there were no further signs of cultivation.

As the great forest closed around us, we felt its immeasurable vastness. The planes and cedars made it most beautiful, very light and airy, but it was full of dangers, and carcasses of mules beside the path reminded us of the presence of savage beasts. Ibexes and wild cats fled at our approach. We walked in single file, the coolies in front. They were barelegged and barefooted. Carrying our bundles on their heads and loads of dry branches for the evening fire, they looked less like men than like beasts of burden. When the light began to fade they lit lanterns, for when daylight goes one feels afraid; the forest is too huge for men to find any comfort therein.

On the ridge, we passed through the ghost of a deserted village where all the huts were barricaded. No booths or shops were open. Only a few cultivated terraces and some stacks of charcoal suggested that it was inhabited. We saw no one. Shortly afterwards, Panditji thought that he recognized a short-cut and we followed a path that soon petered out. Everyone stopped. Panditji, calmly smoking his pipe, ordered a fire and hot tea. He made it quite plain by his tone that any comment would be unwelcome.

Suddenly a man appeared and Panditji called out to him. One of the miracles which Swâmi Vivekânanda describes in his journeys through the Himalayas had occurred for my bene-fit—a man had come out of the thicket at a critical moment to set us upon the right path. It was rather late in the evening when we arrived at a small village, where a Brahmin school-master acted as government agent for the surrounding district. We camped out in the single room that formed his school, and ate our evening meal at his house.

When he received us, the schoolmaster was naked above the waist, with his Brahmin cord across his shoulders. I was irresistibly reminded of the story in the Upanishad of the four hungry travellers, who, all unexpected, knocked at the door of a poor Brahmin's house. He welcomed them, prostrating himself, and giving them his last remaining rice; but the travellers remained hungry. Then he took his wife's portion and that of his father and mother in an effort to satisfy them, and they went away leaving him their blessing. That same night the four members of that destitute family died of starvation, and were received into Paradise by those very travellers, none other than the gods, who had appeared to test their faith.

We, too, were hungry. Poor, the schoolmaster certainly was, but Panditji filled his bare room with high hope of all the benefits that the new India would bring. He spoke of an enlightened socialism, very near to that of the old traditions, that, one day, would find its fulfilment in Parliament itself. The two chelas said little, and I still less.

When Panditji presented me, he said by way of introduction, 'She is on her way to work with Srî Satyakama.' In India, everyone belongs to somebody or something, to a family, a caste, an ashram, or a guru. I, also, had been given my allotted place. No one paid any further attention to me.

That night, the jackals howled without ceasing. I was woken early by the sound of voices and when I lifted the sarî, which enveloped me like a small tent, I saw Panditji sitting by the door in the traditional posture for meditation, before a lighted fire. The two chelas sat beside him. They were reciting Vedic hymns and making ritual oblations.

I was expecting that we should start early, before the great heat set in, and that, indeed, had originally been the idea. But in the forest no one stirs before the principal meal of the day, and we eventually left at about eleven o'clock. In the meanwhile, the schoolmaster assembled the villagers to meet us. Among them were some Doms, small farmers with very dark skins, descendants of those native Himalayan tribes, who still exist on corn, lentils and onions, just as they did in the seventh century. At an even earlier period they had been conquered and enslaved by the fourteen Aryan kings, mentioned in the Vishnu-Purana.[1] They never recovered their freedom, but fled

[1] The Scripture according to Vishnu, one of the most ancient of the Puranas. Probable date, between the third and fifth centuries.

ever deeper into the forest in an effort to hide their gods and guardian spirits. Later other conquerors had come, each more tyrannical than the last. Those from the plains brought mules and ploughs, burning the land and cutting down the forests, building houses, fortifications, and temples in honour of their victories. They laid down cruel laws, terrifying to the original inhabitants. Even to touch a cooking-pot belonging to the victors was made a crime punishable with death.

'We, Brahmins of Rajputana, once seized their lands,' said Panditji, 'now we are making them citizens of an independent India.'

We walked for the whole of that day, but as one of the chelas had hurt his foot Panditji decided to stop at a village where there was a road leading towards the Himalayas, instead of continuing to the Dakbungalow, which the British had built seven miles from Devî-Dhura. As a matter of fact, he was glad of this opportunity of meeting the local corn-chandler, a ragged old man, who in his youth had worked on the plains and therefore spoke English. It was a long time since he had returned to his native village and had taken up his former way of living. He looked as strong as a tree; when his garments fell into holes, he patched them from others, and he never changed them by day or night. 'A tiger', he said, 'does not change its skin.' He was clear-eyed, with much simple wisdom.

We saw women coming back from the forest with nets full of pine needles upon their heads to serve as bedding for the animals. They appeared in groups, looking exhausted, the colour of the earth, as though they were clothed in dust. So poor a village! But I, myself, was little better off, for I, too, was covered with dust from head to foot, and my heels were cracked because the ground was alternately burning hot and icy cold. What is more, we had no precious water to waste on washing. These forests are without streams or springs and the atmosphere is oppressive. Once, indeed, we had passed through a cool, shady gorge where there must have been water nearby, but the men hurried on without saying a word because wild beasts are apt to lurk in such surroundings. Men feel safer on the bare ridges, exposed to the sun and wind.

When we were having our evening meal, the old villager brought wild honey, which he had collected from a nest in one of the trees. He invited us to gather round a fire, burning in a brazier of the correct dimensions—one cubit in either direction—such as is used for ritual oblations. Six men, all from that same village, were already assembled at a little distance. Panditji made them draw near and told them the latest news; the women listened from the doorways. There was no light but that of the moon. Then there followed a deep silence.

Suddenly a man exclaimed, 'Hari Om! Hari Om!' with the full power of his lungs, the words resounding like hammer blows upon an anvil. His voice was re-echoed by the bubbling sound of the communal hookah.

Then the old villager broke the silence, turning to Panditji and asking, 'Maharaj, has God form?' To which Panditji replied, 'That which is eternal has no form, nevertheless that which is eternal has form. That which is eternal dwells in a form that is not eternal. The Eternal can be identified with nothing. It is "eternally changing".'

There followed a long pause. After which the old man told us a story. 'I went up to the top of the mountain. There I met a hermit. I said to him, "Sadhu, where are you living? Show me the altar where you worship God!" I saw his hut, and the stone roof, and the plank bed on which he slept. He showed me his body and said to me, "I am the temple. I have made this 'self' to serve as a temple. Here is where God has made his habitation." '

After a moment's pause, he spoke again to Panditji, saying, 'Maharaj! what have you for me? I am old and soon I shall die. I salute you as though you were my god, sitting by my fireside. These ashes are as fine as dust. Put ashes upon your brow and dust in your mouth, for both represent dissolution—that void, within which the spirit (purusha) endlessly creates.'

Again, he said, 'No temple is necessary for worship. I am nature, I am a tree, I am a flying eagle, I am God in you, and you are God, who has come this very night to teach me this. You needed to come to my fireside so that I might die. When the philosopher's stone touches iron it becomes gold. The Eternal is contained in this moment of time!' And the old man got up and prostrated himself before Panditji, who joined his hands in blessing. Then he rose, and everyone else did the same.

That night I slept in the booth of a cloth merchant, rolled up in my blanket on a string mattress, with the pack-saddles of the mules who journey regularly to Tibet, piled up at my feet. The three men spread their bedding-rolls on the ground. There were two lanterns and we were given a pail of water. It was bitterly cold, for we were nearly ten thousand feet above sea-level.

On the following day the wind got up and the weather looked threatening. As we trudged along, Panditji realized that I wished to speak to him of the events of the previous evening, but he interrupted me. 'It is often better to forget something that one has heard, when it does not concern one,' he said. 'You need to discard what is superfluous in life in order to appreciate the eternal truths. In this connexion', he continued, 'there is a legend that Kasha, the son of Brihaspatî, descended from heaven to learn from a great rishi all the knowledge contained in the Brahmavidyâ.[1] After serving faithfully at his master's Himalayan retreat for ten thousand years, he discovered the secret of life in the space of one second. That same evening he decided to return next day. He prostrated himself before the rishi and bade him farewell;

---

[1] Original truth.

then he went to pay one last visit to all the things which he had learned to know, the trees, the cows, and the birds. Finally, he sat down upon the bench where he had been used to meditate. Devayanî, his master's daughter, followed him there silently and, at last, he turned towards her saying, "There is no more here for me to do."

' "Have you then found what you came to seek? Have you learned all that you desired to know? Do you now understand all things?"

' "Yes," he answered. "No more remains but to bid farewell to you." Devayanî looked at him sorrowfully. "Can ten thousand years of our love be wiped out in a single moment?" she said. "Alas! when you leave this garden, you will forget all that you did not yourself plant in your heart's consciousness." '

I listened to what he said, but my feet dragged as I walked, for exhaustion was overcoming me. The landscape was starkly beautiful. At some time or another we met a Vaishnava sadhu, a worshipper of Krishna. He was dressed in a robe of white wool and hailed us with a loud, cheerful *'Krishna! Hari Bol!'* (Praise to the Lord Krishna), smiling delightfully through his long beard.

'Krishna! Hari Bol!' replied Panditji, then, looking at me, he said, 'You walk as though you were weighed down by your thoughts, like Bhakti (love), a very ancient woman who once came on foot to these mountains from the south of India. She was worn out with living, and beside her plodded two old men, her twin sons, who never left her side. One of them was called Vairagya (renunciation) and walked on her left; the other was Jnâna (knowledge) who stayed at her right hand. She was dreadfully tired. One day when they were in the forest, she came face to face with the Lord Krishna! She beheld Krishna before her very eyes! She ran straight towards him and, in an instant, in Krishna's smile, Bhakti recovered her laughter, her beauty, and her lost youth. Those two ancient men surely could not have been her sons?' Panditji laughed,

'When you appear before Srî Satyakama, let Vairagya and Jnâna take care of your sandals, and run gaily forward to greet purer joys!'

During the two last hours of that day's journey the rain came down in torrents. We put on the thin mackintoshes, which we had brought with us, but removed our sandals. It was very slippery, for the dust had turned to mud, and the climb up the last shoulder of Devî-Dhura was a long and arduous struggle. The coolies grew nervous as darkness fell and swung their lantern, shouting, 'Bhag! Bhag! (panther! panther!),' which made me think of Bhagheera, the slinking black panther of *The Jungle Book,* although I did not manage to see him lurking among the rocks.

The twenty or so houses composing Devî-Dhura and crowning the immense rock of that name, really did look like lairs of the wild servants of the gods, and it came as no surpsise that the name given to Shiva, Lord of the Himalayas, that elusive god who directs the play of life, is Nilikantha (Thou of the Blue Throat). Indeed, Shiva appeared to us at dawn on the following morning, all glorious in that transparently blue atmosphere which is so characteristic of high tropical altitudes. My three Brahman companions invoked him in a hymn of praise:

> '. . . *To Him who is undying,*
> *The Pure, the Space-enrobed,*
> *To Shiva I bow down . . .*
>
> *To Him who is of good promise,*
> *The Rising Sun, Lord of the Blue Throat,*
> *To Shiva I bow down . . .*
>
> *To Him who is the Heart of the Sacrifice,*
> *The Holy One, the Lord of All,*
> *To Him who is Eternal,*
> *To Shiva I bow down . . .'*

The sea of bare mountains that lay before us was suddenly transformed by waves of changing light that reached to the edge of the snow-line. Three white summits, higher than all the rest were illuminated one after another—Parvatî, the Mother-Goddess, rising between the peak of Kedarnath, her temple, and the three prongs of Trisul's trident, which records the variations of the weather. In those icy solitudes legends came alive.

At our feet, the ground had been disrupted by lightning or earthquakes. Five huge blocks of black granite, hurled up from underground, raised uncouth shapes symbolizing the five gods Vishnu, Shiva, Surya, Ganesha, and Shakti, who are united in worship by all the Himalayan valleys stretching down to the plains. In every house and on every roof, pebbles surrounded by a ring of cloth evoke their power and call down their protection. The Gods inhabit the heights of these sacred mountains that face the sky, solitary witnesses of "That which is eternally alive", beyond even the sacrifices which the faithful offer to propitiate the Divine Mother and to win her favour. A few stones under the open sky mark the place where, once or twice a year, sacrifices are made to them, and a buffalo is beheaded with one stroke of a sword.

Lower down, on the other side of the village of Devî-Dhura, there is a temple deep in the forest, not built by men. It is formed of two huge granite blocks propped one against the other—Varahi Devî and Bhim Sen. A cleft between them allows the faithful to reach halls and galleries, hollowed by human hands out of the living rock. This temple of Nature is expressive of simple, yet sometimes obscure, natural laws, which, even at the present time, are not fully understood. Its altars are protected by ragged priests, who admitted even me into the first of the inner courts, pushing and tormenting me to take flowers from their pujâ and to make them offerings of money. They would have been angry, had I tried to enter the dark crypt, where lies the hollow stone that symbolizes the matrix of Universal Creation. Panditji had deputed one of his chelas to protect me and, after their pujâ, they allowed me to process with my friends three times round the sacred cavern, by way of a passage, carved in the rock, from which, far away, one could see torches swung seven times in the darkness of the crypt.

In that rude temple, with its crude symbolical forms, one could readily perceive how for centuries past the Brahmins had excluded all those who did not belong to their caste, and how they had come to lord it over the mountain-people. Nevertheless, in order to retain some contact with the Divine Mother, thus denied to them, the outcaste highlanders have kept up the custom of stroking a particular spot on one of the granite blocks that form the temple, which symbolizes for them the body of the Divine Mother. By their devotion, they have so polished this spot that it has developed a texture as soft as human skin. I saw some of them passionately pressing open palms, then cheeks and foreheads against the stone, as they cried, "Mâ! Mâ!" Mothers lifted their children so that they might touch the sacred place, and, when it came to my turn, I, also, caressed the stone with my hands and said to the Great Mother, 'I, too, have seen you with the eyes of the heart.' The surface of the rock was silky to the touch.

The five Brahmins, who were attached to the temple, acting as priests and caretakers, then came out to join us. One of them was a paralysed cripple. They had the same light complexions as my Hindu friends, and under their ragged clothing, their bodies were as clean, for they observed the same ritual of purification, both inwardly and outwardly. When we left, Panditji laid some silver rupees before the paralytic, who made the sign of blessing. No words were exchanged.

Later, in the forest, Panditji explained. 'That man acts as guru for many souls. Through his austerities, he has unravelled one of the mysteries of Divine Knowledge. He knows one of the direct paths of the Way. He is intolerant and overbearing, but an honest man. He is not the kind of guru who looks after his pupils as a cat does her kittens, nor the kind that gives them the essentials and watches over them from a distance, like the father-fish that swims around his eggs until they are hatched. All that he transmits is the reverberation of certain *bîjas* (holy syllables) which he has gleaned from the *Mantra-Shâstras*,[1] and he communicates this reverberation to those prepared to receive it. That is the only rule he teaches, but he teaches to perfection how to grasp the connection that can bring the inward self into direct touch with the Divine Rhythm. His words strike home, for he understands the four stages by which sound manifests and by which a thought becomes wrapped in the rhythms of the Omkara,[2] before taking definite shape. That man, through the power of his mantras, could cause a tree to germinate or die, for all the elements of nature are revealed to him, as well as the Law that establishes the forces relating them one to another.

'All these things are precisely understood,' continued Panditji, 'and can be passed on to those ready to accept them. But in this life, someone from outside must always come to make the contact between our True Selves and "That which is". After that has happened, an individual may begin to free himself from the grip of his nature. That guru never sees his pupils again, his part in them ends there. He never thinks of them, but none the less he becomes part of their True Being, because they can never forget him. Through him, they are stricken, just as the ground of Devî-Dhura was stricken by lightning, and they know no peace until they break down the barriers to progress which they discover in themselves.'

'But what do you make of all the sufferings that they undergo?'

'Such spiritual suffering corresponds to the scorching, the

---

[1] Or the *Tantrashâstra,* a collection of holy formulae.
[2] The syllable *Om* or *Aum.*

first loosening, of nature's claws. From her grasp we must tear ourselves so that, much later, we may return to her full of grace. When that happens Nature truly becomes our Divine Mother. But there is a long, dark road to tread!'

That evening we spent in the Dakbungalow because the rain had begun again. I overheard Panditji speaking of me to one of the chelas. 'For her, as a woman, the rule is not the same as it is for you. Woman constantly renews herself, for she is creative by her very nature. Her way is to delve ever deeper into herself, and to raise herself to the spiritual state by a graduated series of experiences, consciously lived. For you, on the other hand, the purging fire of asceticism is your only means of refining your nature. Man must live a life of inward austerity if he truly desires to be a man, indeed.'

Immediately after Devî-Dhura the scenery changed, and when we crossed the pass, we saw before us a high plateau to which we climbed by a series of ridges. There was a river! Oh! miracle of water! The forest became full of ferns, moss and orchid-bearing trees. Farther ahead, rice-fields sparkled, reflecting the clouds in their watery surface. There was a new feeling in the air, a delicious sensation as though the earth were sharing in heavenly joys. 'We are re-entering the formal world,' said Panditji, 'but we must be sure that the heart of our True Being is constantly nourished by the ashes of sacrifice. What does my self know, except that my True Self has not yet seen His face.'

When Panditji talked, he deliberately discarded the language of philosophy, so as to break his inclination to paraphrase, and to stay on the emotional level. I had heard him say, 'Do I really know that God exists? Am I capable of following a spiritual rule? My inward self knows only suffering, suffering in waiting for Him to come, suffering in engendering Him, suffering in leaving Him in order to adore Him. Such suffering is nameless. That is what binds me to Him. I am like a blind man who drinks milk; I cannot see its whiteness, but I recognize its taste. Is it possible, Oh! God!, that I may be deceiving myself?'

We reached the river called the Lohabhati (the iron torch), which has a legend accounting for its name. It is said that very many years ago some Brahmans were put in irons by one of the kings of the Chand dynasty, and imprisoned in an abandoned temple that stood beside the river. One day the prisoners were granted leave to perform their ablutions. It was bitterly cold, and a fisherman by the shore had left the remains of his fire. The Brahmins raised their chained hands towards the flame, giving thanks to Agni, god of fire, for his goodness to them. 'Oh! Agni!' they prayed:

'Thou are all splendour and light;
Thou art Brahmah. Thou art Vishnu. Thou art Prajapatî.
Thou art Rudra, Lord of heroic deeds.
Thou art Vayu and Agni. . . .
We bow down before Thee.'
(Bhavishya Purana) [1]

Then the Brahmins went to bathe and, to their utter amazement and delight, they saw that the icy water melted their chains: 'Oh! Agni!' they cried, 'Great is Thy power!'

Sonepur then appeared before us, looking like a nest in that green landscape, so like Switzerland, so far from Europe. Sonepur was the place where Srî Satyakama had his hermitage.

My visit to him was to be a pause in my life's activity, a descent into depths. Where I was going there was no temple, no cloister for novices, no ritual for disciples, no external aids to devotion. That I knew already. The wild Indian jungle that I had travelled through was to be exchanged for the jungle of inward life. Therein the Divine Power, in the shape of various gods, is the force that causes Man first to worship those

---

[1] *The Purana of Times to Come,* a collection of data on the Cult.

gods, then to overthrow and break them, and finally to worship them afresh in a different way, as his consciousness becomes alive to newer knowledge.

I was now beginning to find the silence of my travelling companions oppressive. We spent one more night upon the road, in order to arrive during the morning at the house of a distant cousin of Panditji. There coolies laid down their loads and the party dispersed. I had a bath and put on a clean sarî; then a meal and a siesta. What a comfort that was! The journey had been long and hard. It was not until sundown that we set out for the hermitage of Srî Satykama.

18

Rishida

Srî Satyakama was expecting us. He had sent his servant to tell us so. A mule-path fringed with cactuses led to his retreat. The house appeared suddenly, as we rounded a corner, where a stream flowed into a ferny dell.

Srî Satyakama received us in his own room with many polite attentions, giving to Panditji the seat of honour, the place which evidently he usually occupied himself. Until that time I had seen his face only in the shadow, at Shanti Bhavan; now, I was surprised. There was nothing of the mystic about him, neither in his pose nor in his manner. He looked more like a scholar, in spite of his sannyasm's yellow robe, and it was plain that he had interrupted his work in order to welcome us. He had tea brought, with walnut-kernels, freshly picked almonds, honey in the comb, and fruit, and greatly enjoyed our astonishment at these unexpected luxuries. He was gay and lively, talking continuously and with a kindly smile. There were about a dozen people with him, and I noticed that they all addressed him as "Rishida".

I was immensely surprised to find him in such surroundings. The house, built in the British style, had once been attached to a military barracks, long since vanished. Nothing about it resembled a hermitage. Through the open French windows, I could see flowering yuccas and silver aloes, the trees of a well-kept garden. Another cause for astonishment in that

European setting was that men from very different social levels were sitting together relaxed, their heads resting on their hands, talking naturally and frankly, and eating sweets, while they discussed the harshness of their personal rules. Their total lack of conventionality, their quietness and dignity, created an almost family atomsphere that was illuminated by the radiant face of Srî Sakyakama.

But the moment which I dreaded was fast approaching, when Panditji would leave me there alone. He made a gesture to me to remain seated and withdrew with two or three of the other men. Their bare feet made no noise, but for several minutes we could hear their voices through the trees. Then there was silence, except for the sound of the running stream.

Someone yawned. Only seven of us remained with Srî Satyakama. The servant-boy brought in an oil lamp, which seemed to be a signal, for everyone rose. Then Rishida, my host, showed me to my room that a few days earlier had housed an Englishwoman who had been working with him for the past five years. Rishida, with the same obvious pleasure which he had shown when he gave us tea, pointed out the hanging-cupboard, with hooks and clothes-hangers, the table, chair, and flower vase, all relics of the Englishwoman's ocupation. There was even her wooden bedstead, on which I spread my blanket-roll. The ceiling and the floor of rough-hewn stone showed traces of rat-holes which had been stopped with pebbles and cement.

It did not take me long to discover that Rishida lived in perpetual poverty, almost from hand to mouth, yet, as the Vedic tradition required, all those who lived with him were his guests however long or short their stay. We received everything from his hands, as I learned on that first evening.

Soon after nine o'clock, a bell rang to summon the same seven people to the evening meal. Two copper canteens were brought, each with several compartments, containing rice, potatoes, milk, and hot water. There was also a tray with two bowls for salt and sugar. The meal was eaten quickly, as in monasteries where the monks have the same food always and care little what they eat. Directly it was over we sat in a circle around Rishida. There followed a long pause for mental composure.

Who were these men? They were pupils, passing strangers, disciples whom Rishida had met during his winter on the plains and had invited in the same way that he had invited me. Already, on that first evening, I felt that I had a place among them. They were there because they thirsted for true knowledge, and they spoke without reserve about themselves and their difficulties. There was no discussion. They listed their problems as though making an inventory of their old clothes, and it is not as easy as it sounds to rid oneself of worn-out and old-fashioned clothing. One clings to it. Even though the shape and material is of no further use, one persists in attaching value to it.

Rishida listened to everything with a benevolent smile. Perhaps on my account he took as his text that evening the importance, when one is attempting to transmit deep spiritual truths to strangers brought up in alien traditions, of using a most carefully graduated and controlled series of impressions, and most precise psychological language. Words wrongly used might, he said, prevent real understanding. 'Give yourself up to the forest while you are here,' he then said to me. 'Let Nature do the necessary work in you. Venerate the earth. The forest, the rain, the mountains far or near, have an impersonal beauty that helps to dissolve what we must destroy in ourselves before we can recapture the germ of our thought, the germ of True Being. I, too, am a seeker, I have nothing to give you.'

All those men present had come from far away, from Purî, Calcutta, Benares, even from Assam. They had started their journey in baking heat, and had stifled for nearly thirty hours in third- or second-class railway-carriages before arriving at the foot of the mountains. The last stage, in an ancient motor-bus from the plain at Sonepur, had provided another hazard, for there had been two rivers to ford and an unmetalled road skirting a precipice. During the monsoon season, the only form of communication was by the mules that came up with the mail. The ascent took ten hours.

A first difficulty, which everyone present had experienced, but which none mentioned, was the problem of detachment from the spreading tentacles of everyday life, and of leaving home in spite of all obstacles. This had meant a tremendous effort for all of them, a concentration of their entire selves to serve one aim, to drink, at least once in their lifetimes, from the spring of "That which is eternal", and thus learn to know its flavour. Life at the hermitage was disturbing because of its very simplicity, and still more so because it suddenly aroused a sensation of inner loneliness. The latest comer usually began by chattering unceasingly in order to drive away the emptiness that overcame him. Then, finding that no one answered, he, too, became silent.

That first evening, after the silence that followed conversation, there seemed to come a period when everyone drew a deep breath as after prolonged physical strain. Rishida sat as still as the granite peak of Devî-Dhura, but with the grace and suppleness of one who was not a prey to this world's bitter joys. He remained deep in thought, far away, yet at the same time very close to us, with his hands lying palm-upwards upon his knees. Those hands seemed to contain the whole sum of his experience with regard to the Supreme Goal. By intuition he had knowledge of every living thing in the "sixteen quarters of the universe". How had he arrived at this state? No one could tell. Through intense clarity of vision he both increased the difficulties of everyone there and solved them by his inward contemplation of the Infinite. He looked frail, as though exhausted from having, all through his life, reflected a perfect pattern. His grave benignity, his austerity, all those qualities that made us feel his superiority and deep wisdom, did not prevent him from living with us on terms of rather ironical kindliness, with flashes of amusement in his entire understanding of our various problems. His ways of dealing with us often came as a surprise; for instance, when a few days after my arrival he almost humorously suggested that I should study algebra, as a mental exercise.

The personal relationship which he established with each one of us was unlike that of a guru who leads his disciples to the source of knowledge and gives them rules and a method by which to learn. On the contrary, he simply continued to live his own life radiantly among us before our eyes, and diffused about him the sense of inward freedom to which we all aspired. Except during the hour every evening when he most carefully examined the problems which we laid before him, he lived like a scholar, deeply immersed in his researches. His motto seemed to be "Freedom and Unity".

In the very early part of each morning he worked for the community, himself preparing the principal meal of the day, which the kitchen-boy later cooked, and which consisted of rice, *dal,* and curdled milk. *Dal* was a purèe of lentils with a different taste and seasoning every day, for the gods have so arranged that there are as many different kinds of lentils as there are days in the week. On Sundays we were given as a treat, *kitchuri,* still another mixture of rice and lentils, flavoured with certain spices. Sometimes one of his friends would bring fresh herbs, or carrots and turnips, but those were rare occasions, and fruit was rarer still. Sonepur had neither market nor greengrocer.

We ate at eleven o'clock in Rishida's room. It was our first meeting of the day, and the meal, in spite of its extreme simplicity, was attended by all the Brahmin ceremonies that make eating a sacramental act—purification of the body before the meal, by bathing and clean clothes; purification of intention, by posture and controlled gestures, which make an art out of eating with the fingers; spiritual purification, by which the relaxed mind communicates with the foods that nourish the body and integrates with them. The metal trays, cleaned and polished with ashes, the bowls in which the lentils and curdled milk were served, and the tumblers for the water, were all neatly and meticulously arranged according to precise rules, and each person's place was marked by his particular mat. There was nothing mystical about these arrangements, but they immediately furnished the otherwise bare room, and encouraged our longing for orderliness by overcoming inner rebellion.

Rishida sometimes chose these periods to comment on one of the Vedic Hymns, which he was translating. He would pause at some Vedic root-sound, or at some word in an incantation, which, to him alone, seemed to "come alive through its own reverberation", that is to say, to be the source of a large number of different interpretations emanating from the same sound. Taken out of its particular context, that same root-sound suggested nothing, not even an idea; by itself it had no substance. 'Nevertheless, it exists,' said Rishida, 'try to perceive it as a life-force. It exists both in nature, and in that force which unites one thing to another. You must recapture all its elements and also recapture it in yourselves. When the Creator becomes a vibration for us, then He becomes part of us! Quite suddenly the Spirit is made manifest and embodied. This occurs in a lightning flash, in the drawing of a breath. In any case, time has no length?'

I listened with all my ears, eager to forget nothing of what he said, trying to remember every single word. One day, I took notes, but Rishida laughed at me. 'Why do you want to imprison what I say and give it form?' he said. 'Everything has already been spoken and written many thousands of times. Nothing can belong to you unless it grows within you during a secret winter of hibernation. After that, whatever you remember naturally and effortlessly will be yours, but only after this long testing-time. Light soil catches water and absorbs it.

Baked earth fends off the sun and is carried away or flooded. One day, you will find yourself saying, "I know, I feel, I am." Then it will be true. But you will find nothing of all this in books; truth is written between the lines!'

Not everyone lived in the house. Some slept in the room above mine, spreading their blanket-rolls each night upon the floor; but the rest lived nearby in a corn-merchant's house. The big house was open at all hours to all comers. I was alone there for a week during my first month, after which three other women came for three weeks. None of us became acquainted, there were no farewells when people left. After a time, I asked to be allowed to prepare the evening meal, counting out the handfuls of rice, the two potatoes allowed to each person, and the cups of milk. The boy made a gruel of ground meal, which we ate alone in our rooms before sundown.

19

Frontiers

THREE TIMES, ALREADY, SRÎ SATYAKAMA HAD CHANGED his name. Twice, he had removed to a different province so as to avoid the artificial frontiers with which against his will his friends surrounded him, in the hope of keeping him to themselves. The name Rishida, by which we called him, was reserved at that time for his intimates.

"*Da*" is a suffix meaning "big brother", or "friend". For him, and only for him, it meant the breaking down of a barrier that might otherwise have separated us, for the word *rishi* recalled the Sages of the Upanishads, who, long ago, preached the revealed religious texts. What is more, *rishi* brings to mind a life of austerity, stripped of all social conventions, in which the first step is abandonment of material comfort. Such a renunciation of the habits of everyday life is in itself an overwhelming experience because it means the sudden accession to a new plane of consciousness.

Those who came to learn from Rishida were immediately deprived of all outward forms of worship, and felt that deprivation all the more because of his intellectual austerity. His gentle manner and his silence compelled them to follow their thoughts to the ultimate conclusion. 'Why do you search for words,' he would say, 'instead of expressing your lives by a sense of awareness, by actions that harmonize with your inward selves, and by "That" in you that *knows*. If you still find that you need words, use sentences that contain only twelve. Twelve is a good number, because it has an underlying harmony well worth consideration.' If this had been a game that he wished us to play, we should have found the rules very difficult to follow.

By birth Rishida had been a Brahman of the strictly orthodox type. He had belonged to a most exclusive class. His guests, in one way or another, took a personal pride in that fact and tried to show him marks of respect which he fiercely rejected. He would never allow them to prostrate themselves or to make him the traditional offering of fruit and money, wrapped in a white scarf, that is usually placed at the feet of a guru. Such unconventional behaviour often put his guests and visitors in an awkward dilemma, and they found my presence still more upsetting. I was a foreigner, not a Hindu, yet I handled the evening rice,[1] measured out the milk, and slept in the house. Some of them, with perfect good manners, brought me presents, a small tin of Nestlé's cream or some chocolate, but I could feel their underlying hostility and found it hard to ignore. They had seen me watering the terrace in front of the house and sweeping it, talking to the postman, and attending to the baby of an outcast woman who looked like a wild creature of the woods. From such actions, it appeared to them as though I were either deliberately confusing the normal relationships between people and objects, belonging on different planes, or else that I was a total ignoramus.

Besides being a Brahman of the highest caste, Rishida was also a sannyasin, one of those who lived the life of a hermit after taking the vows of renunciation, obedience to the spiritual law, chastity, and poverty. Rishida used often to say, 'I am a *baül,* which is to say, an independent ascetic belonging to one of the main trends of spiritual life of a period earlier than

---

[1] In earlier times no Hindu would eat food that had been prepared by a stranger.

that of the Vedic religions. In order to keep in touch with the life of the world he was engaged in translating into everyday language some long philosophical works which he thought should be better known. He did this as a useful discipline, knowing full well all that it would entail, and deliberately setting himself a time-limit of four or five years for each book that he undertook, all the while reserving his right to translate in the freest sense. Good sense, unity, and objectiveness, were the standards that he used in his work. The rest of his time he spent in *living* intensively in pure religious experience. His life was simple, poor, and free, without unnecessary clutter. His only possessions were books, and three times already he had given away his library.

The first rains reduced the number of visitors; yet one evening, three travellers staying at Sonepur, Hindu refugees from Pakistan who had lost everything, came to see Rishida. These men were too old to begin new lives. Their sufferings and their dignity hung about them like a garment. They had only one desire left, to receive a blessing from every sadhu whom they chanced to meet and thus find peace again.

From these men Rishida did consent to receive the traditional offerings, and he blessed them when they asked for his, "message". To them he spoke in the traditional language which they expected from him, and he expounded for their benefit the three Sanskrit words, that meant:

> *'Learn to know good from evil.'*
> *'Learn to shun all emotions.'*
> *'Learn to live in the present,*
> *without the past, that no longer exists,*
> *without tomorrow, that is purely imaginary.'*

When they had gone, Rishida said to me, 'For such men these three rules are indispensable, the very marrow of their bones. They have known them since childhood, repeat them automatically, and find them a protection. What they expect from me is that I should repeat them without adding anything extraneous. In the recurring cycle of their natures, amid all their troubles, these three words act like cement in a pavement, unifying them. Such men should have no surface thoughts, no emotional reactions. They should realize that this philosophy is intimately connected with life in all its forms, from the lowest plane, to the high level of consciousness of a Liberated Man. Their faith should be like the scent of the flowers which they offer to the gods.

'But to you, in your present stage,' he added, 'I shall give three different rules for escaping from the everlasting cycle of rebirth. These are they:

"Use the least possible number of objects, for that is freedom from externals."
"Expect nothing from tomorrow, for that is freedom from time."
"Go to sleep each night in the arms of Yama (death), for that is to be reborn each morning."

'When these truths are in your blood, the minutest cells of your consciousness will be transformed.'

The monsoon was about to begin, and for the past few days the weather had been unbearably oppressive, airless, with a desert wind blowing out of Tibet. They say that at such times the men of the High Plateaux see themselves surrounded by disembodied spirits. If that were true, it would not be surprising for under such high atmospheric pressure, blood may spirt from the eyes, nose, and ears. One's entire being, both mental and physical, seems to disintegrate. It is not a question of any yoga of voluntary dissolution, but of some chemical dissolvant acting in the body to separate the flesh from the spirit. A travelling yogi once explained the process in the following words, 'It is a "Discreation" of the whole being, that takes place as the True Consciousness watches the dwindling of the personality.'

At last the monsoon broke. Furious storms filled the valleys with their clamour, like troops of elephants trumpeting and echoing one another from great distances. The forest was covered with flowers, but the grass was full of leaches. The first squalls of wind and hail fell upon us with raindrops so big and heavy that they buffeted our faces. The last of the guests who did not wish to be held prisoner by the mountains left us. On the first evening of the monsoon, I picked up a large bird on the terrace, with both wings broken.

In the months that followed, we lived what Rishida called "the life of modern cave-dwellers". There were four of us left, not including the boy who came for two hours each morning and brought the milk. We were four workers with clearly apportioned tasks. How simple it seemed on the surface! Conditions for working in solitude were perfect. One of us was making a comparison of two Kashmiri versions, published at different periods, of the same document. Another, a Westernized Hindu, was compiling a report for the government, and I was writing the life of an Indian saint. Meanwhile, Rishida was deep in his translation of a Mandal from the Vedas. It would all have been easy had not Rishida introduced a new standard of criticism both for ourselves and our work. Were we, he asked, being 'as true as possible' as compared with the Absolute Truth? That, indeed, was the reason for our coming, but hardly had we begun to test ourselves, than the watery blasts of the monsoon loosed such a tumult upon our minds and emotions that we were all but overwhelmed.

Rishida worked all day long, invisible, unattainable, so impregnable in his smiling silence, that we fled rather than meet him. Towards the end of the afternoon, he seized the opportunity between showers to go for a walk in the forest. He went alone. In the evening, by common consent, our talk was wholly restricted to what we had done during the day, and the difficulties that we had encountered. We all had troubles, for it had taken none of us long to discover that our chosen tasks were no more than projections of our personalities and, at that point, we felt deeply humiliated, all the more so, because in and around us we felt the shining lucidity of the Master.

If any of us showed signs of discouragement, Rishida would quote a passage from the Shâstras: 'Never speak of your spiritual experiences before they have been properly absorbed into your everyday lives and have ceased to affect your emotions. Should you do so, you will only reveal how narrow is the range of your inward selves in your search for self-knowledge. Do not behave like small children, who run to mother about each new discovery. Clothe yourselves in silence. Force yourselves to engender true emotions.'

In the forest, the potent rhythm of prakriti, released by the monsoon, sustained us in our trials. The encircling curtain of rain helped us to appreciate our privilege in being there, and in being able to lead a life so simple that it stimulated our consciousness. Each word, as we uttered it, developed a special intonation that belonged to the Inward Self. 'That is how "The Word" becomes living,' said Rishida, 'the Upanishads are one result. In them, the Spirit has conquered prakriti.'

None the less, we were not yet capable of working like the little jeweller of Sonepur who sang all day in his booth as he wielded his hammer. Rishida cited him to us as an example of a happy soul. The materials that he used were gold, base metal, and a complete understanding of the Law, with which all his very simple actions were harmonized. In him, the craftsmanship of the goldsmith and the artistry of the engraver combined to produce jewellery of great beauty, and he sold his pieces only to people whom he liked personally. This little jeweller was at that time his own best guru.

During the winter months Rishida habitually left his work and went down to the plains. He always kept to the same itinerary, staying for a time in some of the northern towns, then in Benares and Purî, before going on to Assam. Wherever he stopped, a small circle of scholars would gather about him, and for two or three nights running they would sit on the roof of a house or at the bottom of some garden, talking until the dawn. These men were pandits, schoolmasters, or lecturers, eager to study and understand the Upanishads, and they discussed the ultimate problem that is beyond all time, the problem of progressive liberation from the wheel of prakriti. They shared experiences, told what observations they had made as they followed their personal rules, and spoke of the progress of great religious movements in India and the West, as compared with the advance of science and mathematics. They also discussed those trance-states that have been studied earnestly in India since the time of the Vedas, because they provide a practical method of escaping from the endless round, by means of the Enlightened Consciousness. At the borderline of prakriti, self-knowledge, active, stark, and vital, is packed, as it were, into a seed-case, where dwells the perfection spiritual life.

On his journeys, Rishida stayed with friends who, although they themselves were very poor, clubbed together to pay his fare to the town where he was next expected. To such friends, he acted as guide, psychologist, doctor, lawyer, and teacher, all rolled into one. He gave them solid support in their sadhana (religious rule), so that their dream of meeting God face to face might become a practical possibility. All India dreams of *meeting* God! Rishida would say to these people: 'Your piety is very great, but for such a meeting you must prepare on every plane of consciousness. How can grace descend and dwell among us in the midst of the turmoil of opposing impulses? In your inward selves you must light the candle of well-directed effort. Let it reflect the Divine Will, so eager to consume whatever must be destroyed and to transform the residue into something new. It lightens all that is heavy, calms whatever is violent, and revitalizes the senses.'

Rishida sometimes taught in parables, saying, 'Take a broom and sweep clean the courtyard of your house, then sweep out each room, and every dark corner. When you have quite finished, put your broom in the court, where you can find it as soon as you wake next morning, for then you must begin to sweep all over again. Always the dust falls; you must not miss a single day! Guard your broom as though it were a member of your family! Then, "That" which is the true master will stand in the best room to welcome "Him" who comes— and they will recognize one another.'

From the children of his friends Rishida consented to receive the charming acts of veneration which were his due as a sannyasin. Then he would gather them into his arms and tell them funny stories to make them laugh, while he fed them of cakes and sweetmeats from his pocket.

20

The Way of Rishida

$\mathcal{B}$Y COLLECTING VARIOUS SCRAPS OF INFORMATION I HAD gradually come to know the story of Rishida's life, and had written it down. One day I showed him the manuscript, asking him whether I had the facts correctly. 'Yes,' he said, 'all that you have said is true, but what have you gained? Facts in themselves have no importance; many thousands of lives are like mine; thousands of people have felt the call to the religious life and have started out to conquer the Spirit. That is typical of India. A hundred thousand seekers take the road; one, perhaps, may reach the goal. As in Nature, a vast amount of material is needed before one seed takes root. All seeds do not germinate, those that do not, make humus, just as all those who do not find what they seek, help to make that spiritual atmosphere, which is so characteristic of India. No one ever speaks of failure here, for all know that the harsh law of obedience, on every level of self-knowledge, is needed before a spontaneous creation can be engendered. Such is the way of religious aspiration, leading from men's hearts to the higher power, and encountering that same power as it descends into the human heart. When the expansion of the True consciousness suddenly turns inward the strain is over, and the Self lives each moment in perfect communion with God.'

Rishida once said to me, 'I was born in a little village in the east of Bengal. There were thatched roofs and palm-trees, mangoes on the edge of a swamp, and flocks of white storks flying overhead. It was peaceful, like all rice-growing country. I was only twelve years old when the idea first seized me of becoming a sadhu. It came to me in the following way. My father was an intensely pious man. Happening, one day, to open a religious book, he was fascinated by the portrait of its author and there and then decided to seek the writer out and invite him to be our guest. At that moment, I was staying with an uncle in the north of our province, but a letter arrived telling me to come home. I set out immediately, and as I walked straight ahead under the burning sun I found myself repeating, "I am going to see my Thakur (the Holy One who is embodied for me). This is a man who has really achieved the Goal! He is *my Thakur!*"

'When I reached home, I learned that he would not be arriving for another three months, but, as I waited, the glad song continued in my heart. When finally I saw him, I realized that I had not been mistaken. I loved him at once, and something within me exclaimed, "I will give up my life to this man!" Until then, I had never bothered particularly about the idea of God. Like all other Brahmin children, I used to say my Sandhyâ (the ritual morning prayer), and I knew the Gitâ and the grammar of Pânini[1] by heart, but at that precise moment a new idea came to me, filling every part of my consciousness— the idea of serving, loving, and following him. He was *my Thakur!* That stage lasted for two years. My father went regularly to see him, and each time came home a changed man, brimming over with stories which he told to my mother and grandmother. I listened to them in silence, but they took root within me.

'Then the critical moment arrived, for, one night, my father woke me in my bed and said, "In a year's time you will be six-

---

[1] Or the Ashtâdhyagî, which is regarded as a sacred text (fifth century B.C.).

teen and grown up. You must then become head of this family; with your mother's consent, I have decided to go and live at the feet of a guru. Your grandmother will take care of you all. The money for your education has been put aside. You will be a doctor like me."

'I felt as though the ground were opening in front of me. I knew that my duty was to obey, but I also knew that in the end I, too, should go. The struggle lasted for seven months and then, one night, I slipped back the bolt of the front door and left without saying any good-byes. I lived with one idea: *He* is my life. My only desire was to lead the life described in the Upanishads, in natural surroundings, sitting at the feet of a Master, so that I, too, might learn to achieve the Goal.

'My guru lived in Assam, where the government had given away marshy lands infested with malaria to any farmer willing to reclaim them. The tasks which he assigned to himself were the conquest of these wild swamps, and victory over man's inner nature. I had been living with him for several months when the great news arrived that I had won a scholarship. As a matter of fact, I had completely forgotten ever having been a good scholar, but my guru said, "Since that is so, you had better return to your studies. I shall need a man like you, later on!" So I left him for several years and only returned when I had taken my university degrees.

'I then received my initiation as a sannyasin. My guru made me hold my own funeral, when I renounced all that had hitherto been myself, and all that had belonged to my past life —my name and caste, my family and friends, my learning and my thoughts. All was consumed and offered up as a burnt sacrifice. Nothing remained to me but my faith—faith in my guru, faith in the Divine Power, faith in the True Being, which is Perfect Knowledge. My initiation ceremony was a very simple one, according to the Vedic rule. Three times, taking the sun as my witness, I said, "I renounce, I renounce, I renounce." Then the guru prostrated himself before me, because, according to the Law, we were now equals. Symbolically, my only personal possession should have been a rough-hewn staff, but even that he took from me, saying, "If I do not take that away, you will leave me and will not do my work!" Thus I knew in my heart that although I was bound to labour for him in his great work, I was not spiritually bound and that one day I should have to go.

'For a space of fourteen years, my guru laid up on me the burden of working in silence, without news of the outside world, without letters. I helped to cut down trees, dig canals, make bricks, and build houses; such was my daily task. In the evening I taught Philosophy and Sanskrit, and learned to live an inward life meticulously controlled, and thus gradually to possess my True Being by accepting automatic obedience to another. When the soil has been well prepared the tree will thrive. At night, when we meditated, the smoke of surrounding braziers reminded us of all those who were living on the by-products of the trees which we had felled.

'In the beginning we were four disciples living with the Master, but soon we were fifty. In the early years of the twentieth century, India was inspired by the teaching of Swâmi Vivekânanda[1] who, after his glorious return from spreading the knowledge of Vedic thought throughout America, collected together a handful of monks, determined to "till the field of human prakriti". After the death of Swâmi Vivekânanda, independent cells were formed by those who wished to live according to the law of the Shâstras and at the same time serve their fellow men. Religious life found a new mode of expression.

'Our own lives became better organized, for we were now

---

[1] Narendra Nath Datta (1860–1902), the most famous disciple of Srî Râmakrishna, who founded the monastery of Belur, at Calcutta. Many hospitals and dispensaries, schools, colleges, and other social and cultural establishments of different kinds have been founded by the Râmakrishna Mission.

producing all necessities in the way of clothing, food, and fuel. We never had more than one servant, who taught us to saw wood, thrash corn, plough, and reap. Soon we had a school, a dispensary, a monthly newspaper, and annual holidays on the guru's birthday, when all the poor in the district were fed. Ours was a monastic rule. One thing united us, the guru's authority. It was a harsh discipline and we all had moods of exaltation alternating with depression.

'It sometimes happens to one who follows the way of detachment that he enters into the death of his lesser self and suddenly finds himself face to face with his own Divine Essence. Such a one has a sense of the miraculous. He enters into the mystery of meditation, which is ecstasy. He becomes full of the stream of Divine Power. He suddenly brims over. He touches the highest point of his personal evolution, and at that moment cares little whether or not he has attained to the very summit of perfection! On his own level he has mastered Nature and escaped from it. The sensation of being the temple of God possesses him to such an extent that he is able to say, "I am Thou. Thou hast created me, and I create Thee in my image." '

That was where Rishida stopped. Was it then that the guru had said to him, 'Take back your staff and travel on. You are one of those who must create. Live now, and express yourself'? That, I never discovered; but he had obeyed some order and had left. After spending so many years cultivating the land, he disappeared and spent at least as many more cultivating the human race, until eventually he was discovered directing a group of pupils in the north of India. It was then that he began to translate fundamental texts, hitherto almost unknown, and to read them to his friends. That became his official work at one particular period. Then, one day, accompanied by a single disciple, he journeyed to the Himalayas and thenceforward divided his time between retreats and more active work. In both he expressed the True Consciousness by which he had won his freedom. Since he had ceased to teach, people did not at first ask anything from him. But in him silence spoke more loudly than words; for with each new stage of his evolution, his life demonstrated a voluntary retreat from the power of prakriti. All his opposing impulses were transformed into forces disciplined by asceticism. He become impersonal to such a degree that he renounced even his name.

21

Rishida's Guru

RISHIDA HAVING TOLD US SO MUCH ABOUT HIS LIFE, WE felt able to ask the traditional question: 'Who was your guru?'

'He was a man like myself,' he answered, 'in the sense that he had never been tormented by the thought of God. He came to Him solely through love. His parents arranged a marriage for him when he was not yet eighteen, with an extremely beautiful, very young girl, who was also intensely religious, spending whole nights in meditation. My guru often told me that she tried unceasingly to raise him to the level of her own understanding, and that she had been his first Master.

'As is usual in all orthodox Brahmin families, this very young couple had no sexual relations during the first year of their married life. During the second year the husband was sent far away to work on the construction of a canal. He had to leave his wife home.

'One night, as he was asleep in camp, he was awakened by a strange noise. He sat up in bed, and saw his young wife standing beside him, her eyes full of tears. In his astonishment he asked her how she had been able to come to him from so far. Then, as he tried to embrace her, she disappeared, and he was left in such mental agony that it was as though he had been stabbed.

'Next morning he received a telegram announcing her death, the shock of which was so great that it nearly drove him out of his mind. "Since she has come to me after death," he thought, "I must be able to find her somewhere." And it happened that in his search for his dead wife he found God. He travelled from one sadhu to another, hoping that one or other of them would show him the way. He himself then became a sadhu, and wandered about for a long time until, eventually, he met Bema Kepa, one of the greatest gurus of the last century, and told him his grief. Bema Kepa then spoke of the Divine Mother, goddess and mistress of that "void" wherein all things are created, and finally gave him initiation, so that he saw Târâ the Divine (the Divine Mother Salvatrix) and was consoled.

'He did, indeed, see Her, but realized in a flash that She did not represent the whole of the Truth. He had, in fact, been living under an illusion; for although forms reduplicate themselves and die, they are not *That which eternally is.* At that point he began to thirst for knowledge of *That which is,* and removed himself far from Bema Kepa.

'Shortly afterwards, he met a guru from Rajputana, who taught how to attain to the three states, "Pure Being" (*Sat*), "Pure Essence" (*Chit*), and "Pure Bliss" (Ananda), and followed him in his wanderings for the space of three years. While he was with him he ceased to think about his wife, but pursued the narrow way of intuition. His meditations were directed upon Brahman, *That which is Detachment.* The rule of his guru permitted no attachment of any kind. When the Master and disciple arrived in any place, they would build themselves a grass hut and settle down to meditate; then one morning the guru would say, "Let us go!" and before leaving they would burn their shelter. At last, however, the guru ordered his pupil to leave him, saying, "You have learned from me how to know Brahman with your head, but not with your body or your heart. Travel on alone. A Master will come who will teach you what you must know."

'The abandoned pupil searched everywhere for a new Master, until, at last, when he was crossing the jungle that surrounds the Mishmi hills, he lost himself and had to spend the night in a tree. When daylight returned, he looked down and saw a sadhu meditating at the foot. The sadhu said, "I was waiting for you, come with me to my Ashram." That was where he met Sumerdas of the Punjab, who initiated him into the yoga systems applying to the body and senses, and he followed this new guru as far as Tibet and Assam. Then he again set out alone on his journey towards the West, until he met a female yogi, named Gauri Mâ, a very old woman, although she appeared like a young girl. She had a great number of disciples, and was like a mother to him. In her pure maternal love, he found a quiet tenderness that filled him with joy. From that moment onwards, he recognized the face of the Divine Mother in all the women whom he encountered, whether they were young, old, beggars, beautiful, or hideous. Everywhere he turned, Her glorious Beauty was revealed to him.

'His period of asceticism having reached its culmination, he went into the Garo mountains and lived a hermit's life of complete solitude directed by his own knowledge, until some woodcutters found him and suggested his going with them to the family of a Brahmin priest. That was where my father saw him for the first time and, later, decided to follow him with a band of friends, who wished to centre their lives upon his, so that they might learn from his knowledge and experience.'

On another occasion, one of us asked Rishida about his guru's particular teaching. But Rishida dealt with this question by asking another, 'What are you seeking? Do you know? What stage have you now reached? Your question only makes sense if you already know where you stand.'

This conversation was continued when a friend came to visit us. 'The whole of India,' said Rishida, 'follows, in effect, the same spiritual way. But there are as many different levels as there are points of departure. One may remain at some comfortable stage for many lifetimes. In pursuing its evolution, India needs all the strength and all the energy of her children. Time is of no account.

'The first stage on the way is the vow of *brahmacharya,* the vow of continence.[1] The brahmacharya is a beginning of detachment, a vow freely accepted by one who sets forth with a host of ambitions, desires, and impulses, that prove to him the multitude of selves contained in his nature. The second stage is the frank placing of all these different selves at the feet of a guru who, at that moment, represents solid earth, a fixed point, a standard of stability. All these various selves then become unified through the yoga of the guru. The third stage is to project this unified self into everyday life, in close connection with the two fixed conditions of discipline and effort. As soon as a pupil becomes aware of this connection, no matter what level of consciousness he may have gained, a change occurs and his whole being rises to a higher plane. He begins to live; for already he is escaping from the slavery of "names and forms".' Then Rishida talked to us of Juggal Kishnor, who had been a great influence in his life.

'When I first saw him at the Ashram,' he said, 'he was a man of about fifty, with hair as white as snow. He was still big and burly, but his head was bent forward, like Christ's upon the Cross, and he had sad eyes, which he never raised. He was a very quiet man. Round his neck, he wore a chaplet of small wooden beads. In his boyhood he had come from Assam to work as a coolie in a tea-plantation, a slavery not unlike that of the negroes of Louisiana, a black page in the world's history. One's heart bleeds to hear them tell of the things that happened on tea and indigo plantations, for the Law allowed very harsh treatment.

'Juggal Kishor was originally hired for five years, but it

[1] Chastity is only one aspect of the brahmacharya system for directing the True Self on the living plane.

was almost impossible to leave a plantation once one had placed one's thumb on a contract. A man was no longer his own master, and never had enough money to buy himself out. Juggal Kishor married a woman belonging to a different caste, but that was of no importance among coolies; the fellow-sufferers might freely intermarry. The couple lived together in great poverty for fifteen years, and then the wife died, leaving him with a sickly boy of twelve years old who died soon after. At that time, Jugal Kishor became desperately lonely.

'He did, however, manage to regain his freedom, with a few other coolies who formed a small community of independent labourers, not far from Badjo. They were miserable outcasts, but they were free! In Bengal, they have a saying that if a man is an outcast he is bound to be a worshipper of Krishna. And, indeed, since the days of the Buddha, the love of Krishna is the only support to such unfortunates; for he puts into their mouths the Holy Name of one of the gods, that sacred Flute-player, whose other name is Joy. *"Krishna, Krishna bol!"*

'A mendicant, who used to visit them whenever he passed through that district, brought them to the Ashram to sing the bhajans (religious songs) with us. Gradually, Juggal Kishor developed the habit of coming to us, until, at last, he asked if he might remain. He had a mighty work of purification to perform in himself.

'He was a skilful craftsman in everything that he undertook, and was particularly good at building huts of mud and straw. He seemed passionately attached to his work, and wholly absorbed by it; for no sooner did he complete one task, than he left it and set about another with the same energy. No one, however, could read his heart. In his relations with the rest of us he was perfectly submissive and patient.

'One day, he disappeared. But in an Ashram, many people have fits of rebellion, and no one is astonished when that happens. Something had gone wrong, we thought, and he had left us. Two weeks later, however, he returned looking haggard and bewildered, his eyes blazing. He threw himself at the feet of the guru, exclaiming, "I have been rebellious! My soul was in Hell. I could not believe that you were my guru." Then he told us that he had bought a railway ticket for three annas, which had taken him as far as the junction; but when he had arrived there he had gone suddenly blind. "The night came in full daylight," he said, "I could see nothing, neither the train, nor the railway lines. It was because I had deserted you, who are my Master."

'After this crisis, he was again the silent man whom we had first known, and did his work as usual. At that time, I was teaching the Samkhya, in Sanskrit. We held the course very early in the morning, before we went to work in the swamp. Juggal Kishor joined the class, sitting in a far corner, with his head bowed. He never missed a lesson. We used to say to one another, "He does not know a word of Sanskrit; what good can it do him?"

'Then he disappeared for the second time, and we wondered if he had once more run away. We learned, however, that he had gone to one of the farms attached to the Ashram, and that he was safe from harm, doing no work, but meditating, fasting, and silent. When we went to see him, his eyes were red and he seemed completely absorbed in his own thoughts. We feared that he was mad and dying, but we did not know what to do for him.

'He did not die, however, but returned to the Ashram three weeks later, very weak and exhausted. He asked to have a conversation with the guru, a thing which he had never desired before, and they spoke together privately.

'That evening, the guru sent for me and said, "From now onwards take the greatest possible care of Juggal Kishor. Serve him devotedly, for he is one who has achieved the Supreme Goal. There is no one greater than he. He has experienced all the samâdhis (raptures) of the Samkhya. Among all of you, sannyasins and brahmacharins, there is no one to equal him. He is a saint. By pure intuition he has worked out all the lessons and the Law, itself."

'During the remainder of his life, Juggal Kishor did not speak, but his silence became for us a new source of understanding. Without his great rebellions he would never have achieved the Goal. The shocks which he received from them were essentially divine, for he was of the stamp of those who become Masters. He died humbly, but among us he was honoured, as one who in full consciousness "understood".'

22

Work

PANDITJI ARRIVED FOR A VISIT OF FORTY-EIGHT HOURS. We were not expecting him, but he stopped on his way to install a magistrate in the chief town of the neighbouring district. Panditji was one of Rishida's spiritual family, in the same way that I was a member of his own. Our meeting showed me once again how right I had been in going to the hermitage after my stay at Shanti Bhavan. Quite simply, I had travelled a little farther, following the stream of the river of the True Knowledge upwards towards its source. Panditji had done the same, but he had taken a sudden plunge into knowledge deeper than any which I could have hoped to attain at that particular time.

Twenty-five centuries have passed, during which such external events as new contributions to the ideology and systems of the Hindu religion, and the effects of Mongolian, Mohammedan, and Christian conquests, have destroyed the ancient life in hermitages. Nevertheless, the essence still remains, for that is of the Spirit, which never changes. A few may still be found who derive the true essence of Hinduism, that "pure sensation" of the Divine, from the texts of the Upanishads. Contrasting with this abstract conception of the Deity, is the extravagant display of faith that corresponds to the longings and aspirations of a rapidly increasing population. Such faith, though it may cling to tangible aids to worship, also springs from the

Holy Word. It, too, is prakriti, tilling the soil with emotion.

Panditji remained for two days, during which time we went on an expedition that very nearly ended in disaster. We had gone to visit a sadhu who lived on a hill to the north of the town, and on whom everyone in those parts regularly called once a year, bringing presents of money. This holy man, or so they said, had been at least thirty years old when he had first arrived, and that was more than fifty years ago. Yet he never grew older. His teeth, indeed, had fallen out, but his face was quite unlined. He spent his time in prayer and intercession for all who needed help or protection. A servant-boy cared for him and brought him meals of dried fruit and milk. His hut was freshly whitewashed once a year. Rishida said of him, 'This sadhu has succeeded in identifying himself with the mountain, so that he is now one with it. His thoughts are those of the mountain.'

The sadhu blessed us and gave us tea before we started on our way back through the forest, but almost as soon as we entered it we were lost. For about two hours we wandered about, vainly trying to find the path, until we suddenly realized that the sun was setting and that we must, at all costs, reach the road at the bottom of the hill before nightfall. We thereupon decided to scramble straight down the side, clinging to branches and tufts of grass. It was dangerous. There was a bad moment when I covered my face and let myself slide. When we finally reached the road where we thought safety lay, we found two wolves waiting for us. Luckily, we were too big to attack and we managed to drive them away with our sticks. It was by then almost dark and we ran for home, forgetting our bruises and scratches.

On the veranda that evening, we were still feeling the effects of our adventure. It was so quiet that we could hear the sound of the crickets and the whistling frogs down by the stream. There was no light to be seen.

'What does the spiritual search really mean?' said Panditji, beginning to soliloquize. 'On the vital plane we Hindus are like forest trees of different sizes and at different stages of development. Just as the trees are rooted to the ground, so are we fixed in certain essentials of our lives. We have no choice. It has been like this for thousands of years. Our class, environment, and careers are prescribed for us; even our wives are chosen. Thus we are apt to repeat the experiences of past generations, since occupations, opinions, food, education, ritual, and mantras, are all laid down by a tradition that allows no room for free choice. Our traditions bind Man to Nature as closely as the earth is bound to the universe. Can you understand?' he said, turning to me, 'that such conditions are ideal for releasing the Spirit? By compressing us they liberate an energy that finds its outlet only in spiritual advancement. That effort is the only way of breaking the *karma* of repetitive and interconnecting events.'

After a pause, he added, 'I have lived my life faithfully in the tradition of my ancestors, but my sons will not follow my example, because the stream of the Life-Force has changed direction at this period when a Kalpa[1] is ending. The rising generation enters a life that is developing in a different way; the name and form of the impulse may vary, but the primary Law remains the same.

'One deliberately checks the activities of prakriti at every level,' said Rishida. 'A man who lives retired from the world freely chooses to limit his range. By so doing, he is able to preserve all his strength for those disciplines of self-investigation and self-control, on which he has embarked—his vigils, yoga postures and fasts. On the other hand, a man in the world must collect his energies and decide exactly which field he intends to cultivate. In either case, there is a connexion between the discipline and the chosen effort. Spiritual life evolves with

[1] A period between two creations, reckoned at more than four million years.

the degree of harmony between the discipline and the effort.
Like all other births, that of Spiritual life is accompanied by
suffering.'

'What tools do we need to cultivate the field of prakriti?'
one of us asked.

'Only two,' answered Rishida, 'understanding and loving
patience; for Nature's rhythm cannot change. She has three
primary elements: night, when all spontaneous movements
(tamas) are curbed by the darkness; dawn, with its flood of
clear light that inspires Man to act (rajas), and twilight, whose
tranquil glow encourages him to complete his tasks. These
three elements are also in us. They are an essential part of us,
enveloping and influencing us, alternately stimulating and
restraining. They intermingle, merge, separate, or destroy one
another. A true sadhak (seeker), subject to these external
and internal influences, knows no rest once he has embarked
upon the Way, until he achieves the Goal. There are five different levels to attain and he must persevere unceasingly.
Though he may stumble a hundred times, a hundred times he
must pick himself up and continue.

'The sadhak's first task is to study the rhythm of Nature,
without sharing it. Next, he must learn to trust her, so that
gradually, calmly, and smoothly, he may come to know her; he
must learn to love her without becoming enslaved. Finally, he
will control her, or so he will imagine, until the time comes
when he realizes that Nature never changes, but that he, himself, is liberated.

'Nevertheless,' added Rishida, 'the sadhak finds the ascent
to each successive level very difficult, for it is always dangerous
to interfere with Mother Nature (prakriti). There are rules
to be obeyed; one must learn them and not cheat. An old folk-
tale from Bengal illustrates this particular danger. Once upon
a time, a certain man, named Nanda Chand, succeeded in
conquering Nature to the point where he could change at will
into a crocodile. He learned a mantra for that purpose and

often made use of it. The transformation, however, occurred in a flash, so that another mantra had to be ready in order to change him back again. Now Nanda Chand boasted to his wife about this power and she pressed him to demonstrate it before her. First he refused, then allowed himself to be persuaded, and finally agreed. He told his wife to fetch a jar, which he filled with water while reciting the appropriate words that would return him to human form and this jar he carefully placed beside the river. "I am about to become a crocodile," he said ."When you have examined me sufficiently you must pour the water from that jar over my back.' And so saying, he was a gigantic crocodile. His wife, taken wholly by surprise, was panic-stricken and fled shrieking into the house barring the door behind her. In desperation, the crocodile crawled after her and thumped upon the door, but by that time she was beside herself with terror and could not move. Her cries alarmed the neighbours who came running out armed with sticks and stones. What then could Nanda Chand do except crawl back to the river? They say that he can still be heard groaning and lamenting in the night-time.'

On the following evening Rishida spoke of evolution, according to Lecomte du Nouy's system of using figures followed by a number of noughts to denote the passage of time. He quoted from the Vedas, stressing the moments when *The Immobile* developed the power to move, and when *The Mobile* manifested itself by taking name and form.

Rishida hardly ever discussed deep meditation, that state when the physical body becomes perfectly motionless and absolutely relaxed, when thought ceases, or, at the most, is scarcely appreciable. 'At such times', he said, 'there is a strange inward sensation of being, like life in a seed—life with no apparent motion. Consciousness of this sensation for the merest fraction of a second is proof of having experienced what happened when *That which became manifest by taking Name and Form* emerged out of *The Mobile*. Further, and much more remotely, one can then conceive what happened at the moment when *The Mobile* emerged out of *The Immobile*. Such reactions are matters of accurate knowledge; no imagination is of any use in apprehending them.

'During deep meditation', continued Rishida, 'the person who passes from one level of consciousness to another obeys the same law. In a second he experiences "non-existence", that is to say, not being alive. Then, suddenly, he is flooded with such an abundance of life that, purely for that reason, the agonizing question, "Why?" is banished for ever. *"Shanti, Shanti, Shantihi!"* he cries, for that word of peace is pure love. The way of the sadhak is known and well-mapped. When Srî Râmakrishna gave himself up to ecstasies that sometimes lasted for several days; he perfectly realized that at a given moment this flooding in of life would come, to be followed by the re-emergence of familiar sensations at every level of consciousness. No yogi enters into deep meditation without fully understanding the limits of possible detachment and the laws governing the re-attachment of the various elements, so that he may eventually return to ordinary life. But the method cannot be written down or taught because there is no theory attaching to it; it is an actual experience, resulting from a relationship set up between "pure existence (chit)" and something that harmonizes in the person who attempts the experiment. For those who know there is nothing miraculous about it, even although their disciples may think so. It consists entirely in the ineffable fullness of *That which is.*'

My neighbour here interrupted with a question: 'What must we do to gain this knowledge?'

'Study, experiment, and live it as far as possible in your ordinary lives until the time comes when you can absorb it into your own rhythm. The grace of Supreme Love will reveal it to you in time. The flow is continuous between the seed and the fruit. What is written in books does not touch the heart of a reader unless he experiences what he learns. What is taught cannot reach the soul of a listener until he lives what he hears. One can no more pass on the Truth than one can acquire it from others.

'Nevertheless, there is Life of the heart. Speak to your hearts; speak slowly, clearly, *using no words*. Give birth to that Life that lies concealed therein. Feel it! Know it! It is as shy as the turtle doves that perch on the balustrade every morning. Do not hold your breath as you listen to me; do not stiffen your bodies in an effort to understand. Relax, let the stream of Life flow through you as water flows from a spring even after someone else has quenched his thirst there.

'Try to remember everything that you do or touch or see; do not forget; all these things are written in your memory heart, your vital consciousness. Consider your impulses. The most subtle are useful guides that lead to your inmost self once no cleavage any longer exists between body and soul, matter and spirit. If, in spite of all the complications and business of life, you could learn to be as vast as time and space, as light and as transparent as the "void" which surrounds the Divine Mother, She would act for you and disentangle your difficulties. She is a skilful worker, but you never allow Her to help, and you do not know how to withdraw to that "secret chamber" where She dwells.

'Once upon a time', he continued, in that special voice which he kept for story-telling, 'there was a yoginî (a female ascetic) who possessed that power of making herself as vast as space.[1] She lived at the foot of one of the trees in the forest. One day the King saw her when he was hunting and fell in love with her serene beauty. He begged her to return with him to his palace. The yoginî smiled but did not answer. Then the King returned day after day, alternately threatening and imploring, until, finally, he asked her to be his wife and reign with him. She accepted on one condition. "Promise me," she

[1] A key word used to describe an exact state of consciousness.

said, "to give me one room in your palace, and give me the only key. I shall go there every day. Promise never to follow me, and never to enter that one room." Wild with impatience, the King agreed to her request. Thus the yoginî became Queen, and reigned beside the King, covered with jewels in perfect majesty, so that her wisdom became legendary and her fame spread beyond the frontiers of that kingdom. Then the King took umbrage. Becoming more and more jealous of the Queen's great power, he attributed it to something that happened in her secret room, and swore that he would find her out in some disgraceful action whereby he might destroy her. One day, therefore, he went with his ministers and broke down the forbidden door. There was the empty room disclosed to him, and in the centre of it he saw the Queen, in meditation, dressed in her beggar's cloak, and with her hair unbound. Her eyes were full of tears, but her face was radiant.'

23

The Divine Mother

Whenever Rishida began to speak of the divine Mother, he threw himself upon our mercy, for we never tired of listening to him. He had promised to tell us some of the old sacred myths, and one evening when the intimate family feeling in our group was particularly strong we urged him to delay no longer.

The dancing lamps of the fireflies illuminated the night. They made a bright curtain of light, behind which we could feel the darkness full of fluttering wings. We could hear the cries of the owls and the barking of jackals. The air shook with the chirping of crickets. From time to time the cheerful song of the night-birds rang out. Twice, already, we had heard the sharp whistle of the "pilot", that strange feline that acts as a scout for the great hunting tiger. But it must have been a long way off, far on the other side of the river.

'Târâ! Târâ!' said Rishida. 'What a gentle face the Divine Mother turns to us this evening!'

'Have you ever seen her?' one of us asked him.

'Yes,' answered Rishida. 'The Divine Mother, born of Perfect Wisdom, was once revealed to me in the face of a little girl of three years old. She was as white as those virgins who, throughout the ages, have given birth to the "Son of the Spirit" each time that he "needed to come". I asked the little girl to tell me her name. She answered, "I am Atman (the Divine Spirit)", and went on playing with a garland which she was holding in her hands. Her grace was the light of my life for many long years. Such a meeting is an experience that lives in one's heart, and shows the exact level of consciousness to which one has arrived and the distance left to travel.'

In the ensuing silence, we all realized that Rishida's simplicity had broken down any barriers that reason or supposed knowledge might have raised between us. His manner confounded us; for he was very artless, and yet so very downright in his statements.

Later that evening he explained to us on what plane of consciousness an experience may have results vital to the spiritual life, and permanently affecting those who live it. 'There are', he said, 'seven planes, the first three of which are the gunas—ignorance, activity, understanding.[1] These planes are composed of an infinitely complex substance which may be more or less dense, or fluid, and which we have to "work". The potter's hand works the clay, mixes it with water, moulds it and turns it, until a form appears which may be rough, or, perhaps, admirably shaped. That is an illustration of our True Self, inspired by an eager longing to emerge from the darkness, and seeking for the Divine Mother. She, herself, stands at the threshold of the fourth plane, which is that of all possible manifestations. From thence we emerge into the light. How will the Divine Mother appear to us? No one can tell.

'She is the "operative" of the Spirit,' added Rishida. 'India is like some vast factory, from which rises a great cry of supplication, "Mâ-Mâ (mother)". Two main currents sweep the living along; materialism, which now absorbs the youth of India, too long restrained, and spirituality, the renunciation of active life, the call of the Well-beloved, who dwells in the heart. Both these strong currents have fed Hindu religion throughout the centuries, and have endowed a faith in which all Hindus find refuge, even those who appear most Western-

[1]Tamas, rajas, sattva.

ized. The Divine Mother is the Force that sets in motion the three lower planes of changing life. She is the generating power of our bodily and instinctive selves and of our vital and intellectual being. She is also the Force that governs the three higher planes of existence. These are planes of which it might have been impossible to conceive, had not a few sages and great yogis, at different periods in the world's history, crossed the barrier of the Inconceivable. They thus demonstrated that Man may develop beyond his natural plane and that his search for the Divine Mother is justified. These higher planes are those of "Pure Being", "Radiant Energy", and "Joy in Creation". They are the sacred, eternal syllables *Sat-Chi-Ananda,* expressing the ultimate goal of life.

'It is easy to describe the Divine Mother as she appears in her most sublime manifestation, and to think of her as powerful and victorious. It is more difficult to recognize her when she works humbly in our everyday lives. Yet so she may appear at many different times when something, for instance shock or fear, occurs to disturb our inmost selves. One has an instinctive reaction—one bites one's tongue.[1] Whatever is on one's tongue penetrates one's body like lightning. It may be only a momentary fear, but it is a moment of truth.

'At such moments, the Divine Mother is not the goddess seated upon a golden lotus in the sanctuary of a temple, nor the perfect Mother who, for fourteen years in my Ashram, provided an indispensable link of kindness and understanding between myself and my guru. She often takes very humble form, a bride, perhaps, or a daughter-in-law, a woman of the streets, a courtesan, or, it may be, a mountain, a river, or the earth, itself.

'There are well-known legends that help one to recognize Her, but still more interesting are the events which have taken

---

[1] The instant of awareness is often suggested by a Woman biting her tongue. This is the gesture of the Goddess Kâlî in her rapid flight.

place in various families and have been handed down from generation to generation because they have an appeal in every age. Such stories have become part of an oral tradition.

'One of the greatest Masters in Tantrism, who was also a great pandit, lived three hundred years ago in a little village in the eastern part of Bengal. This pandit had a beautiful daughter, but half her body was white, and the other half was dark-skinned. Thus one of her cheeks was as light as day, and the other as black as night.

'That pandit kept a *toll*[1] that attracted many pupils, amongst whom was a certain Ragavananda, a young man of a most uncommon type, very grave and gentle-natured. Without his being aware of the fact, this Ragavananda was a natural yogi. It happened one day that all the pupils of the *toll* went fishing in a certain pond and, before they began, they opened a sluice to allow the water to escape, so that they might wade into the mud and catch the fishes in their hands. They all fished except Ragavananda, who sat gravely watching them. Now the water from another pond drained into the first by a little gully. It began to fill again, and the pupils wished to make a dam, but they had nothing with which to build it. Then said Ragavananda, "I shall lie across the opening of the gully. Make a wall of mud around my body." This was soon done, and they caught so many fish that they could hardly carry them back to the Master. But in their excitement they quite forgot Ragavananda. When suppertime came, the Master said, "Where is Ragavananda?" Then the pupils were seized with fright and ran quickly to the pond to release their friend, whom they brought back all covered with mud, in a deep yoga trance. The Master made no remark. He realized that his pupil had outstripped him in the Way of the Spirit.

'Shortly afterwards, when the school term had ended, Raga-

---

[1] A theological school, where the pupils study Sanskrit and the Holy Scriptures. They are housed and fed by their Master, who begs for them. When they leave, they make him a present.

vananda asked his Master what present he might give as a thank-offering for all that he had been taught, and the Master said, "I have a daughter whom I cherish, but no one will marry her. Take her, and make her happy!" Thus the young man took the pandit's daughter back to his family, who were much embarrassed by her appearance.

'Nevertheless, the marriage was celebrated and, as is customary, on the third day the bride prepared and served many different kinds of dishes for all the members of her new family, gathered around their priest. Now the act of accepting food prepared by her own hands finally unites the bride to the family community; yet the conditions of this particular marriage were such that some of the Brahmin relations decided to refuse the food that she offered. All the guests were sitting in two solemn rows when the young girl appeared, veiled from head to foot, carrying a large dish of rice, which she had cooked for them. Suddenly a gust of wind blew away the veil that covered her face, so that she was seen. There was a general cry of horror, for all had seen her cheeks of different colours and, what was worse, had seen the face of the bride before she had known her husband. At that precise moment, they also perceived two hands joined to a second pair of arms growing out of the girl's shoulders and drawing back the veil to hide a face ineffably serene. Then the entire company prostrated themselves at her feet, for they recognized the Divine Mother and waited for her to bless them as she passed.

'From that day onwards, that young woman was called Ardha Kalî, which means, "Half-Kalî", and the name has been adopted by the whole family who, for fourteen generations, have lived in the village of Mitra, in the Province of Mysimsingh.'[1]

An hour later, Rishida began to speak again. 'Here is another story, which also took place not far from Dacca. It is

[1] Now in Eastern Pakistan.

about a great pandit, named Brahmananda Giri, who lived in the sixteenth century.[2]

'Some Mohammedans had been holding an auction of women in a village of Bengal. Two of them came bearing a litter containing a very young girl, who was about to give birth to a child. They walked upon the tops of the little banks that separated the fields. It was at the season when the jute-reeds are cut down. The girl, who was frightened to death, gave birth to a baby son without the men perceiving it, and she let the child slide down among the reeds.

'Now the baby, whose face had been cut by the reed-stalks, was found by a Brahmin from a nearby village and grew into a fine young man, but he was insatiably passionate and lusted after all the women in the neighbouring villages. He was the scourge of that district. One day he even went as far as the next town to find himself a courtesan, and he discovered one who was very beautiful, although she was already mature.

'One evening, she asked her lover why he had so large a scar on his forehead. "That", he said, "is an old story," and he told her how he had been born. Then the prostitute covered her face with shame and said, "I am your mother! You are my son who has been revealed to me." But the man was terrified and fled, and in his distress he searched far and wide in the province to find a Master to whom he might cry aloud in his resentment. "What sort of goddess", he exclaimed, "is this Divine Mother who allows the rape of a young girl in labour, and permits her son to violate his mother twenty years later? To revenge my mother, I swear that I shall conquer this Divine Mother and make her mine."

' "You are aiming high," said the Master, "and if your endeavours are well governed you may go far. But are you sure that you are prepared to give battle on every plane of

[2] Author of the Shaktânanda Târaginî, one of the Tantrist texts of the sixteenth century. Considered authoritative today.

consciousness in order to win the Divine Mother, for she is hard to please?"

' "So is my vengeance!" exclaimed the young man.

'Then the guru taught him a mantra which, if he persevered, would at length compel the Divine Mother to manifest Herself. Thus, clad in the loincloth of a yogi and with his body rubbed in ashes, the new votary set out, head erect, for the conquest of his Ishta.[1] For years on end, he subjected himself to a harsh discipline in order to become the spirit-witness of his true nature. He inspected the elements and substances that constitute the wonders of the world, vanquished the eleven organs of bodily perception, reception, and expansion, and the five senses of hearing, touch, sight, taste and smell, of all of which he became master. There was nothing that he did not sacrifice in his desire to win the Divine Mother.

'In the beginning of his life of austerity he lived in a grotto, raging against himself, and in his furies breaking the limbs of the forest trees. Then he tried to go back to his village, but the people and the dogs drove him away. So he took to begging in the market places, mocking the people for very shame, and feeding like the goats on rotten fruit and vegetables. His body was full of his mantra, but it had not yet penetrated into his heart.

'At last, one evening, the Divine Mother appeared to him, but she had only one eye. Then the yogi howled in rage, and said to her, "Begone! I want you whole and perfect! Why have you come thus disfigured?"

' "It is not my fault," said the goddess, smiling gently, "if there is a syllable lacking in your mantra."

' "Ah! so you think yourself more learned than my guru, and as powerful as he! You shall see that I shall yet again compel you to come to me. And, next time, you had better be whole!" And he went back to his harsh penances. He knew full

---

[1] The preferred deity of a worshipper.

well that on the day when he possessed the Divine Mother he would achieve in that same moment the highest plane of understanding (Buddhi), that plane where Spirit and body become one and the same.

'More years went by, day was added to day, and finally the Divine Mother again appeared to him, but this time she had only one leg. Again the yogi drove her away. "Begone!" he cried. "I have told you before that I must have you entire to avenge my mother!" The goddess smiled at him. "Oh! my great worshipper," she said, "even though your mantra were perfect, I never could be yours because of my divine nature. Listen to me, however, for I promise to incarnate myself as a young girl whom you may marry, and you shall recognize me. But because you have so much insulted me, remember, that the first time you forget the respect due to your wife, I shall vanish," and so saying, the Goddess disappeared.

'Suddenly the yogi felt that she had gone from him; for her promise meant separation. He lost all his faith, wandering about from place to place like one demented. For fifteen years he vainly sought to find her, but he ceased to importune her with passionate prayer and supplication. One day, worn out with fatigue, he stopped by a well and asked a woman who was standing there to give him water. She was as beautiful as the blue lotus and his heart leaped wihin him—she was just sixteen years old. He obtained her father's consent, then and there, and they married and lived together in a hut beside the river, where he became a ferryman.

'Then, one day, he said to her, "I am hungry and I want fried fish. Give me some!"

' "Alas! I have no fish," said his wife.

' "How dare you say that to me?" said the ferryman, "the smell of frying fish is all about you."

' "It is the neighbours who are frying."

' "I want fried fish," said he. "No matter how you get it, fried fish I will have! See to it!"

'Then to his unbounded astonishment, he saw his wife hold out her hand, and stretch and stretch her arm, until it stretched right through the house-wall of stone and mud and into their neighbour's house, where it took a fish out of the frying-pan. "Do you not know me now?" she said. But his wits had left him and he continued to scold, saying, "How dare you offer to me, a Brahmin, a fish that comes from a weaver's hut?" and he raised his hand to strike her, but the Goddess had vanished.

'Unhappy man! His desire for vengeance was not yet appeased. He devoted his whole life to his mantra and resumed his austerities, so as to compel the Divine Mother to return yet once again. And once more, she came to him. Then, to prevent her leaving him, he said, "Take this rock upon your head, and follow me."

' "As you will," replied the Goddess in her childlike voice. "I will follow you because I love you. But if you stop or turn around, I shall leave you."

'Then the people saw that the yogi walked by day and by night, without ever stopping, and that behind him came a rock, floating through the air. They drew aside from him as he passed, for they thought him mad. At last, at a certain time, when giddiness and exhaustion had overcome him, he no longer heard the tiny steps of the Goddess, nor her anklets tinkling behind him, and he cried out in anger, "Oh! faithless woman, where have you gone! I cannot hear you! Where are you now?"

' "Quite close beside you, almost in your heart," answered the Goddess, and her laugh was like the sound of a waterfall. The man could contain himself no longer. He turned round, but saw only the stone falling to the ground. Then he, too, fell down weeping and broken-hearted.

'Thus, stripped of all his power, he lay beneath a tree in his weakness, and the people passing by succoured him. Gradually he grew stronger and his courage returned. His vengeance was now appeased because he knew the Truth. Then he became a great pandit, a gentle scholar, a man of few words, and every morning, like a little child, he laid a flower upon "The Stone that fell from Heaven", saying "Mâ! Mâ!"

'That "Stone which fell from Heaven",' said Rishida, 'is venerated even today, by many pilgrims to the village of Ramna. It is kept in the courtyard of the temple of the goddess Kâlî.'

24

The Last Lesson

THAT SAME EVENING, A STRANGE THING HAPPENED WHEN we separated for the night, something which I did not understand at that time, but which changed my plans and may have affected the whole course of my life.

Panditji, who had always been most sparing in his gestures, fell at Rishida's feet, face pressed to the ground. I could not understand why he should be taking his leave so solemnly and with such marketed respect, and it pained me to see that tall figure lying stretched upon the ground in the semi-darkness, a gaunt, lifeless mass. He looked broken. We were all shocked at the sight of him. Rishida, who stood facing us, was also taken by surprise. His eyes gazed into the distance, he seemed quite impersonal as he joined his hands in the traditional gesture of salutation and blessing. As Panditji rose, he placed his hand upon his head and said, ' *"That"* which must be, will be at the appointed time. May your way be clear!'

Panditji then exchanged polite greetings with the other two men who were present, and lastly came to bow before me. He placed his forehead upon my feet, saying, 'Didi, may yours be the hands that give me the mother's blessing.'

'May Sakuntala be with you! A good journey to you, Panditji!' said I, deeply moved by his gesture.

Next morning, he set out before daybreak with some other officials. The mules from Kurmachala were saddled ready for the journey, and he called up to me from the foot of the stair-case, 'I forgot to tell you that I am leaving a mule that needs shoeing. They will look after it. A coolie will take it back. *Krishna, Krishna bol!*'

Panditji should have arrived at his destination two days later, but on that day, just as we were eating supper, a mes-senger appeared panting, his face contorted with grief. He spoke all in one breath, 'Panditji Vidyasagar Maharaj is dead. Shiva! Shiva! It happened at the inn last night. He was drink-ing tea, when he was seized with a shivering fit and collapsed. But he pulled himself together, saying, " *'That'* which must be is now, but I want to meet it standing." He died at once. I hurried back to tell you the news. The others will telegraph to his family today, when they reach the town.'

As I listened, I felt utterly shocked, 'This cannot be true! Why? Why?' I murmured. It seemed unendurable, impossible, absurd even, that he should die at the age of forty-seven, leav-ing his wife, his mother, and four young sons.

I tried to catch Rishida's eye, in the hope of understanding, of having something to cling to. But not a muscle of his face moved. He gazed at me calmly and said, 'Why should Panditji not die? For death surely comes to all who are born, as it is written in the Gîtâ.' His quiet, compelling voice filled every corner of the room and stilled my resentment. But I felt my heart desperately crying out for Sakuntala, Ganthu, Mataji. My head was in a whirl, and I suddenly had the impression that every tree in the forest was weeping with me. I could almost hear them sobbing. I felt the blood throb in my veins. But my Self—where was I then? Was *I* transported by that great wave of sorrow? No, for although I heard the sound of weeping, it was not *I* who wept.

No one had moved; there had been a suspension of life, a stillness of death.

Then I began to speak very fast. 'I must go to Sakuntala at once. I must leave tomorrow. I will take the mule that he left behind. I will go with the messenger and the coolie. I must go to them.'

That night we stayed for a long time siting on the veranda, in the light of the fire-flies and the stars. Rishida had shown me a glimpse of eternity when, by his calmness, he had controlled my emotions so that my True Self had been neither assailed nor overcome. It had become like an enveloping cloud, exactly the same shape as my physical body, a light and delicate mist, through which I heard the echo of my thoughts that endlessly repeated, 'Sakuntala has lost everything; she has lost everything!'

Rishida's voice interrupted, as though in answer. 'Sakuntala has lost nothing. The pearl-oyster of the sacred legend leaves her bed at the bottom of the sea and rises to the surface to receive the rain when Svâti is in the ascendant. She floats wide open upon the face of the waters, until she is sent a drop of the miraculous "rain of Svâti". Then she sinks back to the floor of the ocean and there remains until she has transformed that drop into a perfect pearl. What need has she any longer of her shell? Panditji had already heard the "call". When he left us he knew that he was going to meet Yama (death). He received him upright, in a last impulsive leap towards that perfect vision of the Truth, which is Divine Understanding. Can you realize Panditji's loneliness when he was so close to heavenly raptures and yet so bound to his family? He was at that frontier where love understands all things.'

As I listened to Rishida, I felt my tears at last begin to flow, but they were tears of gratitude: Rishida! Panditji! Love! Eternity!

That night I slept peacefully after packing and cording my tin suitcase, and on the following morning I left. Rishida came with me as far as the river. He gave me nuts and honey to eat on my journey. He, himself, was due to leave in two or three weeks' time. How sad that I had to go first, for the last remaining days would have been very lovely, very full for me! But the sense of having to pay a debt drove me on; the flow of life was bearing me away.

When we reached the little bridge, I joined my hands, and so did he. That was all. There was *"That"* between us which must be, and which will be at the appointed time. That truth was bathed in a marvellously clear light.